Basic computer skills
Made Simple
XP edition

Jackie Sherman

MADE SIMPLE
BOOKS

AMSTERDAM • BOSTON • HEIDELBURG • LONDON • NEW YORK • OXFORD
PARIS • SAN DIEGO • SAN FRANCISCO • SINGAPORE • SYDNEY • TOKYO

Made Simple is an imprint of Elsevier
Linacre House, Jordan Hill, Oxford OX2 8DP, UK
30 Corporate Drive, Suite 400, Burlington, MA 01803, USA

First edition 2004
Reprinted 2004, 2005, 2006

British Library Cataloguing in Publication Data
A catalogue record for this book is available from the British Library

ISBN-13: 978-0-7506-6137-9
ISBN-10: 0-7506-6137-2

For information on all Made Simple publications
visit our website at http://books.elsevier.com

Printed and bound in *Great Britain*

06 07 08 09 10   10 9 8 7 6 5 4

Working together to grow
libraries in developing countries

www.elsevier.com | www.bookaid.org | www.sabre.org

ELSEVIER   BOOK AID
            International   Sabre Foundation

Basic computer skills

Made Simple

XP edition

Contents

4 Extra Word features   43

Preface

Although it may seem that everyone else can use a computer and enjoys keeping up with the latest developments, you are certainly not alone if you are new to computers or have some anxiety about information technology.

Sometimes it's the jargon that can put you off, or instructions that are too complicated. Authors of computer manuals may not have actually worked with new computer users and so don't know that it's often the little things that spoil the whole learning experience. This book aims to demystify computers and show you how you can gain the basic skills needed to have confidence and use your computer in exciting and fun ways.

You may have just bought a machine, or need to learn how to use one for work. Perhaps your children are bringing home IT projects and would like your help, or you may want to spend some time e-mailing friends and family abroad or shopping on the Internet for the bargains that are increasingly advertised.

Whatever your motivation, this book will explain what computers are all about and explore the most common applications. With its help, you should be able to produce word-processed documents, prepare illustrated slides to aid your talks or lectures, store and search for information systematically, and handle numbers and charts.

It will also show you ways to access and search for information on the Internet and send and receive e-mails.

Once you have learned the basics, you can turn to other books in the Made Simple series to discover the full power of the applications you have been using.

The examples in this book: they are taken from a computer running Windows XP and Microsoft Office XP, as these are now widely in use.

1 Introducing the PC

Hardware

Although this book won't concentrate much on technical aspects, it helps to know a little about your machine so that you can look after it properly and understand terms mentioned later.

The parts of the computer that you can touch and move around are referred to as *hardware*. The components of most importance are shown in the following diagram:

Extra hardware items, *peripherals*, can be added. They include:

Printers – either black and white or colour

Scanners – to allow you to use ready-printed images or written material in your work

Digital cameras – for transferring your own photos into the machine

Other items such as speakers, microphones, DVD players and CD-RW drives for saving documents or music onto optical disks.

- ❑ Screen also known as the monitor or VDU.

- ❑ Main unit housing processors, memory (RAM) and the hard disk (normally the C: drive). It has a Power On button, and a Reset button for re-starting without turning off the power.

- ❑ 3 ½" floppy disk drive (normally the A: drive) – the slot for a floppy disk on which you can save your work.

- ❑ CD-ROM drive (usually the D: drive) – the sliding drawer for a CD-ROM used to play music or games or install new programs.

- ❑ Mouse – controls a pointer on screen that is used to give instructions to the computer.

- ❑ Keyboard – for entering text and numbers and an alternative way to give instructions.

Software

The programs that give your computer hardware its instructions and which control everything you see on screen are known collectively as *software*.

Systems software

Starting up when you switch on, checking connections and controlling peripherals such as printers, setting the screen dimensions and colours and allowing you to save or access your work are all activities controlled by systems software. The programs are normally stored on the hard disk inside the main unit.

Applications software

This is software installed on your computer for a particular purpose and is independent of the operating system. Familiar applications include Paint, Word and Internet Explorer.

Applications are commonly installed from a CD-ROM inserted in the D: drive and are then stored on your hard disk. However, the files you create using an application such as Paint or Word can be stored either on the hard disk or on a floppy or optical disk inserted in the appropriate drive.

Working with software

In Windows, each application is run inside a *window* – an area of the screen that can be controlled independantly. You can have several application windows open at the same time and can arrange these in different ways on your screen. To give commands, instead of typing in some obscure programming code, you select from understandable *menus* or pictures of objects – *icons* – found inside the window or on buttons on the *toolbars*.

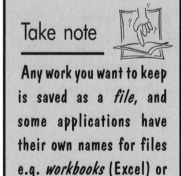

Take note

Any work you want to keep is saved as a *file*, and some applications have their own names for files e.g. *workbooks* (Excel) or *documents* (Word).

Icon on toolbar button

Open menu

Menu item

Controlling the mouse

For something to happen, you need to give the computer instructions. This can come through pressing keys on the keyboard, e.g. press [Enter] to move the text insertion point down a line or [Delete] to remove an item (see page 25).

Some of the time you will use the mouse. Roll it gently around on its mat to move a pointer across the screen. When the pointer reaches the target – perhaps a menu option or an open window – you can either press a button (known as 'clicking') or hold down a button and 'drag' the item to a different position. (In this book, 'click' means press the left button; 'right-click' means press the right button.)

The shape of the pointer changes depending on what action it will perform, and you must take care that it is the correct shape before you click or drag. It can be an arrow, hand, cross or vertical beam and the differences will be explained as you go through the book.

Basic steps

1 Roll the mouse gently on its mat.

2 Guide the pointer until it rests over the target item on screen.

3 Hold the mouse steady and click the left button once, to select an object or choose an option.

Or

❏ Click the left button twice very fast to dou-ble-click and open a window, file or folder

❏ Click the *right* mouse button to open a short menu of options

❏ Hold down the left button as you drag the pointer to move items across the screen

Tip

Double-clicking takes practice. You can often avoid it by select-ing an item with a single click, then pressing [Enter].

Basic steps

☐ Shut Down

1 Click the Start button (start) in the bottom left-hand corner of your screen and select Turn Off Computer.

2 At the dialog box, select Turn Off.

3 Your machine should turn off automatically.

Like any piece of equipment, a computer needs to be treated properly to offer the best service. That means that certain basic rules need to be followed.

Starting

If the computer is turned off, press the Power On switch. You will need to wait for the system to complete its startup routine.

If the computer is shared with others, you may be asked to log in by entering a username and password before you can start work.

A computer that is turned on may show nothing on screen when in power-saving mode, or moving images rather than the normal Desktop – the screen saver. To get back to the opening screen, press any key.

Shutting down

Never switch off the power in the middle of your computer session as you can leave the files in a mess and you'll have to wait next time you start while the computer tidies them up for you. Instead, follow the proper shutdown procedure.

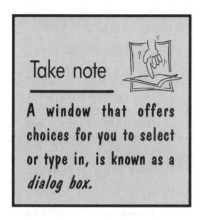

Take note

A window that offers choices for you to select or type in, is known as a *dialog box.*

2 Select Turn Off

Restarting

Unfortunately, the computer can sometimes behave badly. It may 'freeze' so that nothing happens when you try to click the mouse or use the keyboard, or the picture may blur or strange windows may open when you haven't done anything.

In these circumstances, it is often best to start again. Without turning off the power completely, you can restart, or 'reboot', the machine and re-open Windows, or just close the particular application you have been using.

Tip

For details of the keyboard see page 25.

1 If the computer is not responding, hold down the [Control] and [Alt] keys with one hand and press [Delete].

2 Click End Task in the Windows Task Manager dialog box to return to the Desktop. Reopen the application and you may recover your work.

3 If you prefer, switch to another task, or start a new one.

Take note

If you start the PC with a disk in the A: drive the PC will try to find its startup instructions there, and won't be able to. Remove the disk and press any key to start up again.

Basic steps

1 To select an icon, click the left mouse button once when the arrow is directly over it.

2 To open into a window, either double-click the icon or select it and press [Enter].

3 To move an icon on the screen, select it, then hold down the left button with the pointer over the icon, and drag it to a new position.

The Desktop

The opening screen is referred to as the Desktop, as visible icons include common office items such as a wastepaper basket (the Recycle Bin) and you can add others such as a document folder (My Documents).

Desktop icons represent some of the applications, files and folders within the computer. You can even create your own icons as shortcuts to applications or files you commonly use.

Programs, folders and files all open out as windows that allow you to view their contents and can be moved or resized.

Along the bottom of the screen at all times is the Taskbar. This shows the Start button, needed to launch many of your applications; information such as the time and date; certain shortcuts and any open programs or files in the form of named buttons.

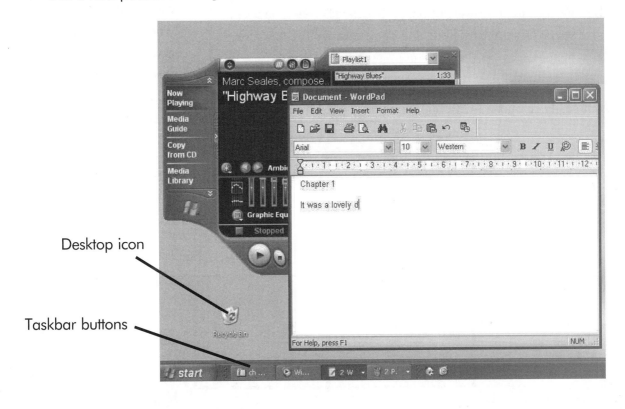

Desktop icon

Taskbar buttons

Working with windows

To work with a window you need to recognise the basic parts:

Title Bar: this shows the title of the open file, folder or program

Menu Bar: this is where you'll find menus you can open by clicking the menu name

Toolbar: click the buttons for common actions

Status Bar: this may show certain details, e.g. about the contents of the window.

Scroll Bars: drag the slider or click the arrows to move the window contents horizontally or vertically.

Control buttons: use them to close or resize the window

To close a window, click ⊠ **Close**.

To resize the window, switch between the two interchanging buttons next to the **Close** button: 🗗 **Restore Down** reduces the size so the Desktop is visible; and 🗖 **Maximize** fills the screen completely.

To reduce the window to a button on the Taskbar, out of the way but easily re-opened with one click; click 🗕 **Minimize**.

❑ To change a window manually

1 Click the Restore Down button.

2 To resize, click and drag any edge or corner in or out when the mouse pointer moved gently over it changes to a 2-way arrow.

Or

3 To move a window, click in the Title Bar when the pointer shows a white arrow, hold down the mouse button and drag to a new position.

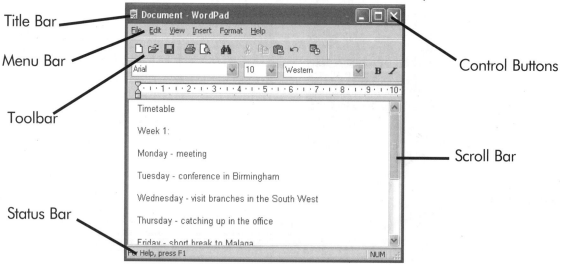

Title Bar

Menu Bar

Toolbar

Status Bar

Control Buttons

Scroll Bar

8

Customising the Desktop

Basic steps

1 Select Start > Control Panel. Click the Switch to Classic View link in the left panel.

2 Activate the Display icon then click the Themes or Desktop tab to set the background.

3 To change the screen saver, click the Screen Saver tab then click the arrow by the Screen Saver box to drop down a list of choices.

4 Select a title to see a sample, and click Preview to run it. Move the mouse or press a key to exit.

5 Set the Wait time to elapse before the screen saver comes on, or set options such as text or colours by clicking the Settings button.

6 Click OK to save your settings and close the Properties dialog box.

The Taskbar displaying the **Start** button is always visible as it is so important when working with the computer. Clicking the **Start** button offers various choices – to launch an application, to find a file, to turn off your PC, to get help on Windows, to run a program e.g. from a CD-ROM, or to change basic settings.

When you select **Control Panel** from the **Start** menu, one option is to customise the look of your Desktop. The Control Panel can be run in Classic or Category view. We will use Classic view as it gives easier access to the controls. You will see icons for various items such as Date/Time, Keyboard, Mouse, Regional Settings and Sounds. Double click or select and press [Enter] to open any item. A Properties dialog box will appear where you can alter the settings.

Display allows you to change colours or show patterns or pictures that form the background to your Desktop, or choose from a range of moving images, *screen savers*, which run when you temporarily stop working.

3 Click the Screen Saver tab

4 Preview a screen saver

5 Set the Wait time

6 Click OK

Opening an application

If you have the appropriate icon on the Desktop, double-click to open the application. Otherwise, find it listed amongst the programs on your computer. The programs that you have used most recently will be listed on the initial Start menu display, but any program on your PC can be found in the All Programs menu system. Open each menu in turn and work through them until you reach the application. A final click will launch the program.

1 Click the Start button at the bottom left of your screen.

2 If the program is listed in the initial display, click on it to start.

3 Click All Programs .

4 Slide across to the next menu and select an application e.g. Microsoft Word, or an option e.g. Games to open a further menu.

5 Click on the name to start an application.

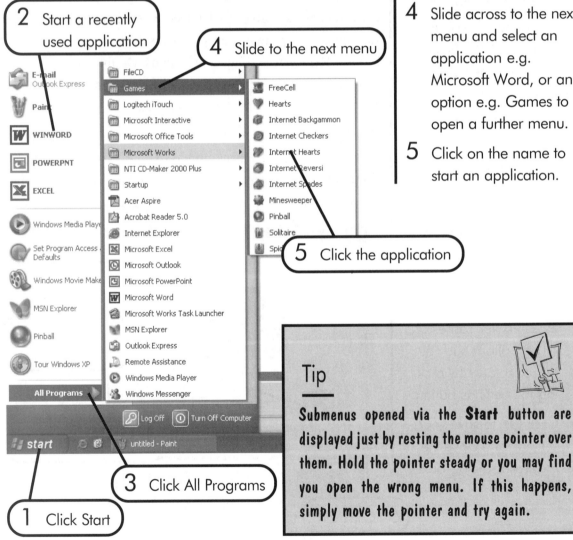

2 Start a recently used application

4 Slide to the next menu

5 Click the application

3 Click All Programs

1 Click Start

Tip

Submenus opened via the **Start** button are displayed just by resting the mouse pointer over them. Hold the pointer steady or you may find you open the wrong menu. If this happens, simply move the pointer and try again.

Looking after yourself

Taking care of your PC

- ❑ Avoid eating and drinking near the keyboard, as liquids and sticky crumbs will ruin its efficiency.

- ❑ Keep any cables or bags well out of the way, so there is no tripping up as you rush to the printer or to answer the telephone.

- ❑ Shut down the machine correctly, rather than turning it on or off like a light switch.

Tip

If you still have trouble after taking sensible precautions, do see your doctor or optician.

When working with computers, there are simple rules to follow that will minimise any risk to your health.

Get comfortable

Make sure your chair is at a comfortable height and supporting your back, and adjust the monitor so that your eyes are broadly level with the top of the screen. If you can, make use of document holders, footstools or wrist supports to aid your comfort. You may also want to ensure you have plenty of room to move your legs freely.

Take breaks

Take frequent, short breaks to stop yourself sitting too long in one position.

Watch your eyes

Adjust the screen or window blinds to reduce glare, and stop working if you get a headache or fuzzy vision.

Adjust equipment

Try to keep a light touch on the mouse, position the keyboard so that it is comfortable to use and keep a good working space round you. Adjust screen settings using buttons on the monitor for maximum clarity and restful colour contrast.

Summary

❏ Any parts you can see and touch are computer hardware whereas sets of instructions written as programs and stored on disks are called software.

❏ The opening screen is called the Desktop and it displays small icons representing the programs and files in the computer. Each program runs in a window that can be re-sized and moved using buttons or the mouse pointer.

❏ You can customise your Desktop via the Control Panel, and find programs from the Start menu, opened by clicking the button at the bottom of your screen.

❏ You should always shut down the computer properly, rather than simply turning off the power.

❏ It is important to take sensible precautions when working at the computer, to maintain your health and safety.

2 Getting organised

Where's that file?

After working on a computer for even a short time, you could well have saved a number of pieces of work, known as *files*, on disk. Each time you want to find a particular file, you'll have to scroll through a growing list of names – a time-consuming and inefficient system. Instead, you can group your files into labelled folders, rather like drop files in a filing cabinet, so that all you need do is open the relevant folder and search through a limited number of files to find the one you want.

You can either manage your files using the File and Folder Tasks or work directly with the folders in the Explorer Bar . Whichever system you use, you can create as many folders as you need and then move or copy files between them.

The folders structure

A disk is known as the root directory or folder and is represented by the disk drive letter. (C:) represents your hard disk and 3½" floppy (A:) represents a floppy disk in drive A.

Folders and subfolders form a hierarchy, or the branches of your directory/folder 'tree', so that a folders structure can look something like this:

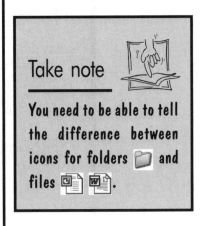

Take note

You need to be able to tell the difference between icons for folders and files.

14

Exploring folders

1 Open My Documents and click the Folders button to display the folder structure in the Explorer Bar.

2 Select the disk or folder in which to create the new folder.

3 Go to File > New, click Folder and wait a few seconds.

4 When a new folder appears in the right pane, type a name into the box to replace the words *New Folder*, and press [Enter].

❑ Made a mistake? Select the new folder and then *right*-click to produce a short menu. Select Rename and edit or retype the name.

In Explorer, you'll see a window with two panes – in the left the folders structure of your computer, and in the right the first level of contents of any selected folder. The Title Bar shows which folder is open at any time and you can click the name of a folder in either pane to view its contents.

If items have + next to their name in the left pane, it means they contain folders. Click the + to expand the structure. Click the symbol again (now –) to return to the root folder.

Creating a folder

Select the location in the left pane (you may need to click + to reveal a particular folder) and then use the **File** menu options to create your folder.

1 Click Folders

4 Enter a name for the new folder

2 Select the disk/folder to hold the new one

Click to close

Click to open

Filing

Once you have created one or more folders, you can reorganise your files *as long as they are closed* – i.e. you are not working on them at the time. If you see a message saying a file can't be moved, return to the application and close the file before continuing.

Files are moved by dragging them from their original position to the new destination. You can also create a copy of a file in a different folder using this method.

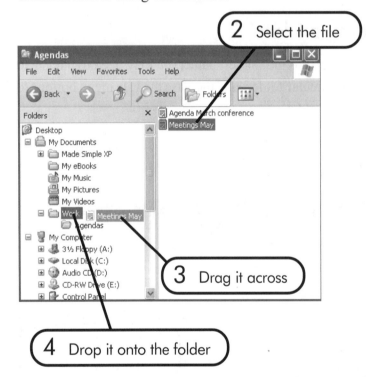

2 Select the file

3 Drag it across

4 Drop it onto the folder

1 Make sure that both the file and the destination folder are visible.

2 Select the file.

3 Right-click on the file and drag it to the destination folder.

4 When the destination folder becomes highlighted, let go the mouse button.

5 Select Move Here to move the original file or Copy Here to place a copy in its new folder.

Take note

It is easy to open a file from Explorer instead of selecting it. Just close the file and return to Explorer by clicking its Taskbar button.

Selecting several files at once

❑ Selecting a range of files

1 Make sure your files are displayed as a list. You can do this by selecting View – List.

2 Click the first file.

3 Hold down [Shift]and click the last file in the range.

All files will now be highlighted.

❑ Selecting non-adjacent files

4 Click the first file.

5 Hold down [Control] and click the other files individually.

6 Drag any file across to the left pane and they will all move together.

To move several files at the same time, you need to use a method that allows you to highlight more than one at a time.

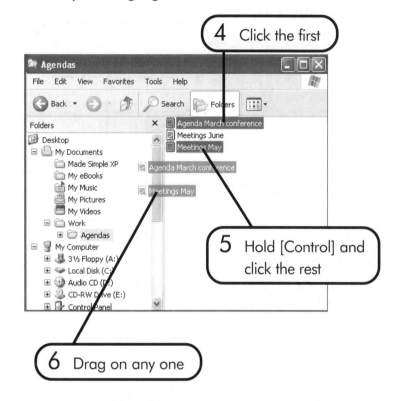

> 4 Click the first

> 5 Hold [Control] and click the rest

> 6 Drag on any one

Take note

If you drag with the left button down, there is no menu when you drop the file. You will always move files within the same drive and copy files between different drives. If you aren't careful, the file can disappear into the wrong folder and you'll need to find it and move it out again.

Folders on the Desktop

It is sometimes simpler to organise folders and files using the File and Folder Tasks that are listed in the left-hand pane when My Computer first starts.

1 Start My Computer and open a folder

3 Type a name

2 Click Make a new folder

4 Go up a level?

5 Copy the selected file

6 Select the folder

❏ To create a folder

1 Click Start then click My Documents and open the parent folder.

2 Click Make a new folder from the File and Folder Tasks.

3 A new folder will appear. Type in its name and press [Enter].

❏ To move or copy files

4 If you need to go back up to a higher level folder click the Up button ⬆. Select the file(s) to copy or move.

5 Click Copy this file or Move this file from the File and Folder Tasks.

6 Select the destination folder in the dialog box and click Copy or Move.

Basic steps

❑ To delete files

1 Select the file or folder and press [Delete].

Or

2 Select the file in the right pane and drag it across to the Recycle Bin folder.

Or

3 Right-click the file and select Delete from the menu of options.

❑ To backup files

4 Select the file(s).

5 Right-click the file(s) point to Send To then select the backup disk.

Tip

To delete a folder, first check that it doesn't contain any files or subfolders you wish to retain. If it does, move these out first and then press Delete.

Deleting files

Files or folders that are no longer needed should be deleted to keep your disks tidy. Deleting is quick and easy, and if a file is deleted by mistake, it can be restored to its original location by opening the Recycle Bin, selecting the file and clicking **Restore this item**.

Backing up work

It's important to keep copies of your work elsewhere, in case the original becomes corrupted. If you normally save files onto your hard disk, keep backup copies on floppies or writable CD.

Either use the File and Folder Tasks option or right-click a file and select Send to, then click the relevant destination. With large files, first send them to a compressed folder, then copy that to your backup disk.

Compress large files

5 Right-click, point to Send To then select the backup disk

19

Viewing files

When you open My Documents or any folder, you will see its contents displayed in the window. You can change the display by selecting different views. Thumbnails will show all your pictures, and Details will display the size, date and type of file that has been saved. You can sort your files by date, name, size or type to help you locate a file quickly.

Double-clicking on an image file will take it into the picture viewer so that it can be edited or viewed more clearly.

❑ To display files

1 Open the View menu, or drop down the list next to the View button.

2 Select a display option. A black ● will appear next to your selection.

3 To re-order the files, select Arrange Icons by and click an option.

❑ To view pictures

4 Double-click a thumbnail picture to open it in the Viewer window.

5 Amend the size, delete, print, edit or copy the image using the appropriate toolbar buttons.

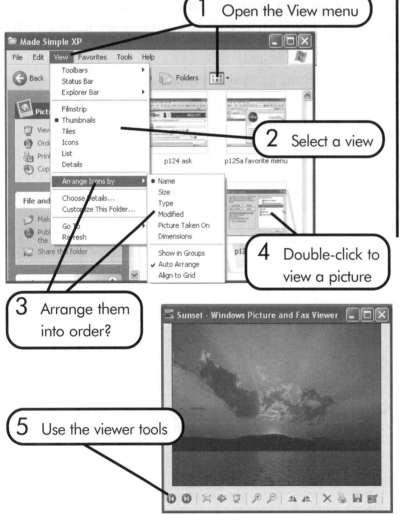

1 Open the View menu

2 Select a view

p124 ask   p125a favorite menu

4 Double-click to view a picture

3 Arrange them into order?

5 Use the viewer tools

Tip

In **Details** view you can arrange files in order of any of the columns. Click on the heading once to list them in ascending order, and again to list them in reverse order.

Basic steps

1 Push the floppy disk into the A: drive until you hear a click. The release button will pop out.

2 Open My Computer and select the 3 ½ Floppy (A:) icon then go to the File menu and select Format, or right-click on it and select Format.

3 In the Format dialog box, leave the options at their defaults.

4 Click Quick Format if you only want to to remove files from an old (formatted) disk.

5 Click Start and wait for the confirmation that formatting is complete. Click OK.

6 Click Close to close the dialog box or repeat with a new disk.

Formatting a disk

Before you can save your work onto a floppy disk, it has to be formatted. This lays down the tracks and sectors for storing information correctly. Although you can buy floppy disks ready formatted, sometimes you may need to use an unformatted disk. You may also want to reformat a disk as a quick way to erase unwanted files. As formatting destroys any information previously stored, you only format a hard disk for special reasons – and only after backing up all your data.

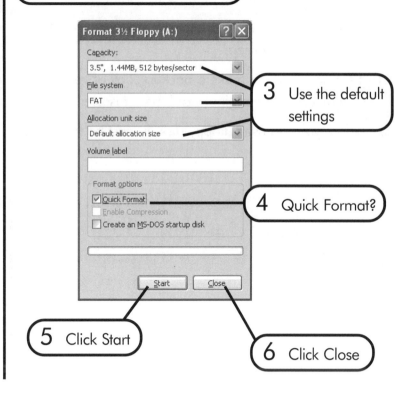

2 Select Format for the Floppy

3 Use the default settings

4 Quick Format?

5 Click Start

6 Click Close

Summary

❑ Unless you organise your files when working on the computer, you will find it very hard to keep track of everything you produce.

❑ Folders allow you to group similar files together so they can be easily located. You can create folders using the File and Folder Tasks or with Folders displayed in the Explorer Bar.

❑ Files can be dragged into folders or placed there using the File and Folder Task options. You can select groups of files to move at the same time.

❑ Take care when deleting folders as they may contain files you want to keep.

❑ It's a good idea to make a backup copy of your work so that losing the original won't be a disaster.

❑ Before you can use a floppy disk, it must be formatted.

Tip

There's more on organising your files, and lots more on other aspects of Windows in *Windows XP Made Simple* by P.K.McBride.

3 Simple documents

Opening Word

When you launch Word, the first *document* (the name given to any file produced in Word) always opens directly on screen. It has '*Document 1*' as a temporary title until you save and name it with a more memorable name.

To open subsequent documents, click the *New* button ▢, or go to **File** > **New** and select *Blank Document* in the Task Pane.

You can open new documents one on top of the other. The names of all open documents other than the top one will appear as buttons on the Taskbar and you can click any button to switch to that document. It will then become the active window.

White space left for page margins

Click to open menu

Ruler

Control buttons

Task Pane

Cursor – the position for text entry

Status bar shows information about the document

Click for more buttons

1 If the Word icon **W** is on your Desktop, double-click it or select it and press [Enter].

Or

2 Click Start, point to All Programs and then click Microsoft Word.

3 To close a document, click the Close button or select File > Close.

4 To close Word, click the Close button still visible, or select File > Exit.

Take note

Only items used often are displayed when you open a menu. To see all items, click the down arrows at the end of the list.

Basic steps

1. Press a key to enter a letter, digit or lower symbol, e.g. / or =.
2. Hold down [Shift] to enter capital letters or symbols at the top of the keys, e.g. + or @
3. Press [Caps Lock] to enter a line of text in capitals.
4. Erase text errors to the left of the cursor with [Backspace], and to the right with [Delete].
5. Press [Tab] to move the cursor across the page in jumps of 1.27cm (0.5").

Entering text

When a new Word document opens on screen, you'll see a flashing vertical bar – the cursor – positioned at the top left-hand corner. This is where any characters you type will appear.

Tip

Only press [Enter] to start a new paragraph. Otherwise, allow the 'word wrap' facility to move text onto a new line when the right margin is reached.

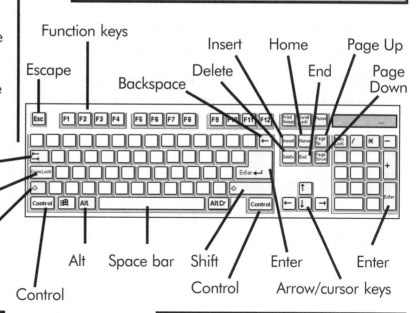

Function keys
Escape
Backspace
Insert
Delete
Home
End
Page Up
Page Down

Tab
Caps Lock
Shift
Control
Alt
Space bar
Shift
Control
Enter
Enter
Arrow/cursor keys

Take note

The apostrophe ' is a lower symbol under @.

Take note

In this book, menu choices are shown in **bold** and keys in [square brackets].

Moving the cursor

Once you have entered some text, you may need to move to different parts of the document to make changes or add new words.

Using the keyboard

- **[Enter]** will move the cursor onto the line below, creating a new blank line.

- The **[arrow keys]** will move it in any direction except below the last line of typing.

- **[Home]** takes it to the start of the line.

- **[End]** takes it to the end of the line.

- Hold **[Control]** as you press **[Home]** or **[End]** to go to the start or end of all text that has been typed.

- **[Page Up]** or **[Page Down]** will move through large blocks of text in long documents. You can also click the vertical or horizontal scroll bar arrows in the appropriate direction.

Using the mouse

When the pointer shows a vertical **I**, position and click to place the cursor on the screen. If it is not in exactly the right place, use the arrow keys to move it across one character at a time.

❑ If the cursor is at the start of a line, pressing [Backspace] will join this sentence up to the line above.

❑ If the cursor is at the end of a line, [Delete] will join this sentence to the following line of text.

❑ Take care not to split words when you press [Enter] as everything following the cursor will move onto the next line.

Click here to start new paragraph

One sentence is short. **I**Two sentences can be longer.

INew paragraphs are hard to cre**I**ate and easy to split up by mistake.

Click here to split the word

Click here to join sentence to line above

Basic steps

❏ Undo

1 To undo the last action taken, select Edit > Undo or click the Undo toolbar button ↶ *before* clicking another button or pressing any key.

2 For mistakes made further back, you can step through the changes you made or select past actions from the drop-down list produced by clicking the arrow next to the Undo button.

3 Select Edit > Redo or the Redo button ↷ if you go too far.

Everyone presses the wrong key at some time, or makes another mistake that could involve a great deal of re-typing, and so Word gives you useful shortcuts to put things right.

Correcting common mistakes

- **Undo** toolbar button allows you to go back one or more steps and is particularly useful if you delete or move text by mistake.

- **[Insert]** key will return to inserting text between letters if you changed to Overtype mode by accident and find text being replaced.

- **Close** button will return to your work if you opened a new document or dialog box by mistake. This often happens when holding [Control] rather than [Shift] as you type a capital letter (e.g. [Control] + [N] opens a new document, and [Control] +[P] opens the Print dialog box).

- **View > Toolbars** or **Ruler** allows you to locate missing screen items. If a new toolbar appears as a box on screen, click in the blue title bar and drag it up just above the ruler or just below the bottom of your document. When you see it start to lengthen in shape, let go and it will spring into place.

Task Pane

This is displayed when you open Word and offers a range of shortcuts for opening and starting documents. It is also used for some other operations, such as inserting clip art. Close the pane via the View menu or its own Close button.

Spelling and Grammar

You may notice that some words you enter become underlined in red or green. Red means Word doesn't have it in its dictionary – often, but not always, because it is misspelt – and green means that it appears to break the conventional rules of grammar.

To check a single word, right-click to drop down a short menu. For selected text or the entire document, click the Spelling and Grammar toolbar button. This will pick up the first underlined word(s) and you can select an alternative, ignore all suggestions or manually alter the words concerned.

1 Right-click on the red or green wavy underlined word.

2 To check the whole document, click to open the Spelling and Grammar dialog box.

3 Select an alternative in the Suggestions pane or edit the mistake.

4 Click Change so that your document will reflect the changes.

5 New words will appear until the checks are complete. Either ignore or alter/replace each one in turn.

6 To leave the checking box at any time, click Cancel.

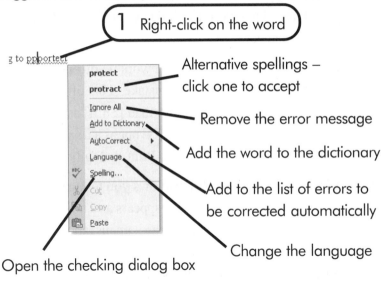

(1 Right-click on the word)

Alternative spellings – click one to accept

Remove the error message

Add the word to the dictionary

Add to the list of errors to be corrected automatically

Change the language

Open the checking dialog box

(3 Accept a suggestion)

(4 Click Change)

(6 Click Cancel to quit)

28

Basic steps

1 Type a question or keywords that describe what you want to know into the box under the control buttons and press [Enter].

Or

2 Select Help > Microsoft Word Help, or click the toolbar button 🔢 or Press [F1] to open the main Help window. You can then select one of three tabs: Contents, Answer Wizard or Index.

3 Select Help > Show Office Assistant to get the helper. You can type questions or accept Help on activities such as writing letters.

   Click the Options button to change the appearance or remove the Assistant altogether.

If you have problems, or want to learn something new, Word has a range of help functions available on-line. You can view demonstrations, have your questions answered, display definitions, get step-by-step guidance, trouble-shoot or simply read about most aspects of the application.

1 Type a question

Contents – select a topic to display in detail

2 Open the Help window

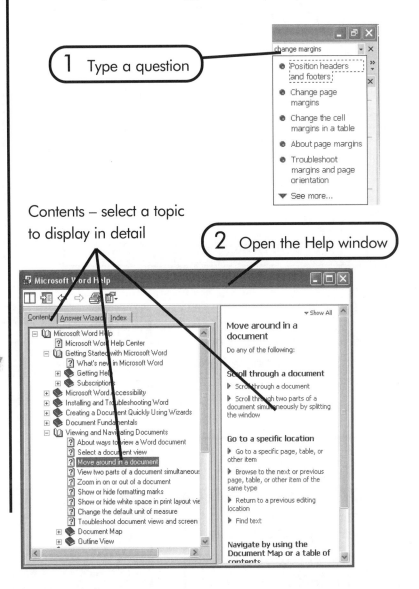

Answer Wizard – type in questions, click Search and select related topics that you can then display

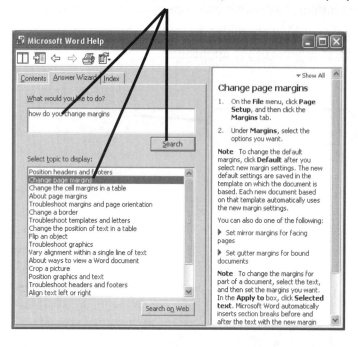

4 Also on the Help menu is *What's This?* Click on this then click a part of the window to reveal a definition.

5 On some dialog boxes there is a ❓ question mark next to the Close button that works in the same way as *What's This?*

6 Select Help > Office on the Web to connect to the Internet and access extra Help and guidance.

Index – enter keywords and click Search or choose from the list to display topics containing those words

Basic steps

Using the mouse

- ❑ Select one word by double-clicking it.

- ❑ Triple-click to select a whole paragraph.

- ❑ To select a block of any size, click at the beginning of text, hold down the button and drag the cursor across to the end.

- ❑ Select a line by moving the mouse pointer in the left margin until it shows a right-facing arrow. Click, or click and drag up or down to select several lines at the same time.

Each document has pre-determined settings that are known as the *default*, and these include style and size of characters, line spacing, margins and the alignment of entries on the page.

To alter the look of your text, either change these settings before typing, or type the text in the normal way and then go back and make changes to particular sections using the various formatting tools available.

To restrict the changes to certain words or paragraphs, you must select (highlight) them so that the text appears white on a black background. Any new instructions you give the computer concerning changes to characters or paragraphs will now only affect the selected text.

There are many different ways to select entries, using either the mouse or the keyboard.

Click here to select the whole line

Selected text

Tip

Select the complete document by pressing [Control] + [A] or go to Edit > Select All.

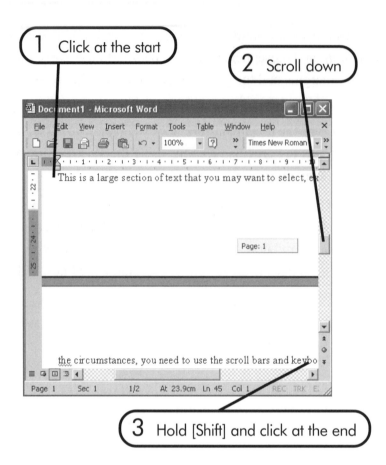

1 Click at the start

2 Scroll down

Document1 - Microsoft Word

This is a large section of text that you may want to select, e...

Page: 1

the circumstances, you need to use the scroll bars and keybo...

Page 1   Sec 1   1/2   At 23.9cm   Ln 45   Col 1   REC   TRK   E...

3 Hold [Shift] and click at the end

- ❏ To select a large block
- **1** Click at the start of the entry to place the cursor in position.
- **2** Scroll down to the end of the block.
- **3** Hold [Shift] and click the button again.

Using the keyboard

- **4** Move the cursor to the start of text.
- **5** Hold down [Shift].
- **6** Press the arrow keys in the desired direction.

Tip

If the black highlight extends too far when selecting text with the mouse, keep the button depressed as you slide the mouse slowly back up the line of text.

Tip

If you press a key when text is selected, it is deleted or replaced with the newly typed character. If this happens, click Undo.

To take off the highlight but not delete the entry: click on screen once with the mouse.

Basic steps

- ❑ Click the toolbar buttons to apply bold, italic or underline.

- ❑ To change the font type and size, click the down arrow by the boxes to display a menu from which to choose.

- ❑ Click the arrow next to the Font Colour toolbar button **A ▾** to choose a colour other than black.

- ❑ Styles combine pre-set font and paragraph settings. A range of styles is available from the drop-down Style list or in the Styles and Formatting Task Pane.

Formatting text

Formatting means changing the look of your text. There are various toolbar shortcuts for applying different formats to characters. Sometimes they can be clicked on and off (e.g. **Bold** or *Italic*) or one format must replace another e.g. font (character design) type or size.

Either set the formatting to apply to the text you are about to type, or select existing text and then apply the formatting.

Styles and Formatting Task Pane

Style   Font   Size   Italic   Bold   Underline

The menus show how the text will look if the style/font is applied

Tip

To copy the formatting that you have applied to some text, use the Format Painter ✐ button. Select an example of the formatted text, then click ✐. The pointer will now show a paintbrush. Drag this across text to apply the same formatting.

The Font dialog box

To make detailed changes to the look of your text, you need to go to the **Format** > **Font** dialog box.

2 Set the font, style and size

3 Pick from the drop-down lists

4 Tick checkboxes?

5 Click OK

Preview your choices

6 Set as the default

1 Select the text then use Format > Font to open the dialog box.

2 Select any font type, style or size and pre-view the effects in the Preview pane.

3 Use drop-down menus to apply special under-lining or text colours.

4 Click in the checkboxes to apply special effects such as shadows or outlines.

5 When you have made your choices, click OK.

6 If you would like all your future documents to have these formats pre-set, click Default... and then click Yes.

Tip

If you type capitals by mistake, select the text and hold down [Shift] as you press [F3]. You will be offered a repeat of lower case, Sentence Case or UPPER CASE as you press. Other-wise, select the text and then go to **Format > Change Case.**

Formatting paragraphs

Basic steps

❑ Setting alignment

1 Click the appropriate alignment toolbar button.

Or

2 Use the keyboard shortcuts:

[Control] + [L]   Left

[Control] + [E]   Centre

[Control] + [R]   Right

[Control] + [J]   Justify

In computing, 'paragraph' means any text typed between two [Enter]s on the keyboard. If you want to format a single paragraph, you select it by just clicking somewhere inside. If you want to apply a new format to more than one paragraph, select the relevant block of text with the mouse or keyboard before formatting.

There are toolbar or keyboard shortcuts for changing text alignment, line spacing or indentation, but you can also make these choices via the **Format** menu.

Alignment

One of the most common changes you are likely to make is to the position of text on the page. There are four alignment toolbar buttons:

- **Left** aligned to line text on the left margin

- **Centre** aligned to position text around a central point

- **Right** aligned to line text up on the right margin

- **Justify** will 'stretch' text across the page and so neaten the right-hand edge. Sometimes too many spaces are inserted, but it can give text a more professional look.

Line spacing

Normally, new lines of text appear one below another with little white space between them. This is *single line* spacing and is the default setting.

If you want more space on your page, you can change to 1.5 or double spacing, or select a specific spacing measurement.

2 Set the Line Spacing

Indenting paragraphs

You may want a paragraph to be set some way in from the left or right margins, e.g. so that it stands out or as a way to present quotations in a document.

This paragraph is not indented and so lines up with both the left and right margins in the normal way.

> This paragraph is indented by 0.5" (1.27cms) from the left but not from the right, so that the application of word wrap always leaves a space on the left.

> > This paragraph is indented by 1.18" (3 cm) from both the left and right margins.

□ Line spacing

1 Hold down [Control] as you press [1] for single, [2] for double or [5] for 1.5 spaced lines.

Or

2 Click the arrow next to the line spacing button and select an option.

□ Indentation

3 To move a paragraph in from the left margin by 0.5", click the In-crease Indent toolbar button.

4 Reduce the indent by clicking the Decrease Indent button, showing the arrow pointing in the opposite direction.

Basic steps

1 Select Format > Para-
graph and click the
Indents and spacing
tab.

2 To change left or right
paragraph indents,
select the box and alter
the measurement by
clicking the up/down
arrows or typing in an
exact figure.

3 Click the drop-down
arrows to see the Line
spacing options and
select a standard spac-
ing or choose Exactly,
At Least or Multiple and
enter the number in the
At: box.

4 Preview the changes
you make and then
click OK.

The Paragraph dialog box

If you want to set your indents or line spacing more exactly, you
can do it from the **Paragraph** dialog box.

1 Go to Paragraph >
Indents and Spacing

You can set the
alignment here

2 Set the indent
amount

3 Set the Line spacing

Use the Preview as a guide

4 Click OK

Tip

The arrows in measurement boxes move numbers in
10ths, but you must click in the box and alter numbers
manually to change measurements by 100ths.

Saving work

After all the hard work of creating a document, you'll want to save it. There are three questions you need to ask:

- Where do you want to save the file? On the hard disk, or perhaps onto a floppy disk or CD that you can take with you to work.

- What do you want to call it? When you want your work later – to edit it or print a copy – finding **Technical CV** is going to be far easier than finding **Document 26.**

- Do you want more than one copy? If you need different versions of a CV, for example, you could edit the original and save both **Technical CV** and **Management CV** files.

1 Click the Save button 🖫 or select File > Save or Save As to open the Save As dialog box.

2 Select the target folder from the Save in drop-down list.

3 Word names files by entering their first line of text into the File Name box. Edit or replace this name as appropriate.

4 Click the Save button.

5 To keep your original unaltered but create a second copy, use File > Save As to open the Save As box and change the location and/or rename the file before clicking Save.

2 Select the Save in folder

4 Click Save

3 Edit or replace the name

Tip

Once you have named a file, save it *regularly* by clicking the Save button, so that you do not lose later work if the PC crashes. This will resave the file with the same name.

Basic steps

1 Click the Open button ☞ or select File > Open.

2 In the Open dialog box, make sure the correct folder or drive shows in the Look in slot – if necessary, look in different folders by clicking the Up One Level button or opening a folder visible in the main window.

3 Scroll through your files and select the one you want to open.

4 Click the Open button or press [Enter].

Opening previously saved files

The main reason for saving files is so that you can open them again later – perhaps to make changes or to print a copy.

If your work has been saved properly, all you need do is open the *Open* dialog box and scroll through your files until you find the one you are looking for. Select it and click **Open** and it will appear on screen as the active window.

2 Select the Look in folder

3 Select the file

Go up a level

4 Click Open

Tip

When transferring files to a different computer, you may find you cannot open your documents because the machine is running an earlier version of Microsoft Word. To cope with this, save your work in a different format by selecting file type, e.g. Word 6.0 or Rich Text Format, from the *Save As type* box.

Print Preview

When typing and editing, it is hard to get a feel for the look of the finished piece of work. Check your work before printing as this is the only way to discover that everything is squashed in one corner, or one word has just gone over onto a second page!

To preview work, view the document in Print Preview. Zoom in on details, correct basic spacing errors and then print directly from here or close and return to the Normal view.

To carry out document editing, click the Magnifier button to turn off Zoom mode. A cursor will appear on screen and you can now alter spacing or delete text in the normal way.

2 Set the Zoom level

Turn zoom off to edit

4 Set the page display

Shrink to fit

2 x 1 Pages

6 Click Close

1 Click the Print Preview button or select it from the File menu.

2 Set the magnification by altering the percent-age in the Zoom box.

3 Switch between this setting and 100% zoom by clicking on the page when the pointer shows a magnifying glass.

4 Click the Multiple Pages button and select the number of pages to see by clicking and drag-ging the pointer across the squares.

5 To see the next or previous pages, press the Page Up or Page Down keys.

6 Click Close to return to Normal view.

Tip

Shrink To Fit can pull back text that has gone over the page. This will reduce the font size but only works for a small amount of extra text.

1 For one copy of your document, click the Print button 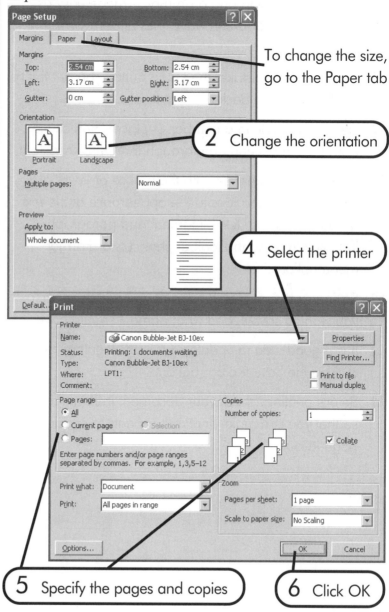.

2 To alter default settings, select File > Page Set up to change paper size or orientation.

3 Select File > Print to open the Print dialog box.

4 Select the printer in the Name slot.

5 Enter the number of copies, and either click Current page or type the page numbers in the Print range area to specify which pages are printed.

6 Click OK.

You can prepare the page for printing via **Page Setup.** The default prints documents on upright A4 (Portrait) and you need to select Landscape Orientation if you want the longer edges top and bottom. You can also select different sized paper on which to print.

To change the size, go to the Paper tab

2 Change the orientation

4 Select the printer

5 Specify the pages and copies

6 Click OK

Tip

Print long documents on both sides of the paper by selecting Print: *Even* pages, then replacing the paper and printing *Odd* pages.

Summary

- ❑ When entering long sentences, you can leave word wrap to move text onto the next line whenever the right margin is reached. To start new lines or paragraphs, however, you must press [Enter].

- ❑ Correcting spelling and grammar is made easy as Word puts red or green wavy lines under words that need checking.

- ❑ If you make a mistake, the Undo button can put things right by stepping back one action at a time.

- ❑ Help is available in a number of places, particularly from the Help menu and through the Office Assistant.

- ❑ If you first select entries with the mouse or keyboard, you can make changes to the appearance of the text or to line spacing, text alignment and paragraph indentation using the toolbar shortcuts or Format menu options.

- ❑ Saving work is straightforward if you are clear where you want to save it, and what name it should have.

- ❑ It is a good idea to update your work regularly by clicking the Save toolbar button.

- ❑ Before printing, check your document in Print Preview so that you can make final adjustments to spacing and page layout.

4 Extra Word features

Pictures

A quick way to improve the look of your work, or clarify a point, is to add a relevant picture. Although you can use an application such as Paint to create your own pictures, or download wonderful images from the World Wide Web, for most of us its easiest to select from the supplied clip art.

A shortcut to the Clip Art Task Pane is located on the Drawing toolbar, but you can also reach it via the **Insert** menu.

Once you have inserted your picture, you can change its size and position and even alter specific details such as colour and orientation using the drawing tools.

1 Click where you want the picture to go then click the Insert Clip Art button 🔲 or use Insert > Picture > Clip Art.

2 In the Insert Clip Art Task Pane, type your keywords in the Search text box.

3 Narrow the search by selecting the collections from the Search in box.

4 Click Search.

5 Click a picture or its arrow, or right-click, then select Insert to add it to your document.

Take note

Many clips will only be available from the Office CD-ROM.

Basic steps

□ Resizing a picture

1 Click to select it.

2 Move the pointer over a sizing handle where it will show a 2-way arrow and drag the border in or out.

3 Go to Draw > Text Wrapping to set how text fits around the picture. Select an option such as Tight.

4 Select a Draw > Rotate option. The handles will be replaced by white circles and a green circle will appear at the top.

5 To move the picture on the page, drag it when the pointer becomes a 4-way arrow ✛.

6 To rotate the picture, drag on the green circle. The cursor will be a circular arrow. The picture will rotate around its centre.

Making changes

A *selected* picture shows a black border and small boxes – sizing handles – and in this state can be resized. It can also be deleted by pressing the **[Delete]** key, or realigned using the alignment toolbar buttons.

A picture can be treated like a drawing object. To position it on the page more exactly, use the tools on the Drawing toolbar.

1 Click on the picture

2 Drag the handle

Dotted line shows new size after dragging

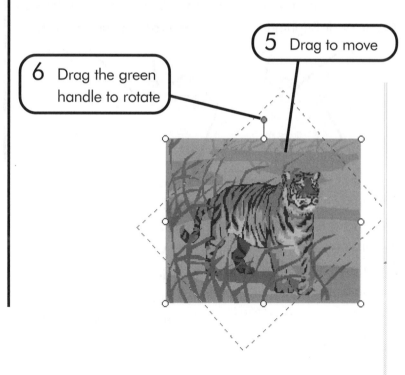

5 Drag to move

6 Drag the green handle to rotate

Editing a picture

To make more detailed changes to your picture, right-click to open the editing menu. You will now be able to add a border or caption, change the brightness or colour and generally customise the picture in a range of different ways.

3 Edit

5 Show the Picture toolbar

Click up or down to change Contrast or Brightness

Text Wrap – controls the way text wraps round the picture

Format

Reset Picture – click if you don't like the changes you have made

Image Control – produce a black and white or greyscale picture or display it as a 'watermark' (pale image) in the background

Click Crop and drag a sizing handle inwards to remove an unwanted area

1 Right-click the picture to open the short menu.

2 Select Borders and Shading to place a border round the picture, or Caption to add a title.

3 Edit Picture will place the picture in a frame – the Drawing Canvas. If it is a drawn clip art picture you can add, remove, move, resize or recolour individual parts within the frame.

4 Select Format Picture to make precise changes to measurements or add a background colour.

5 Select Show Picture Toolbar for a further range of shortcuts.

Basic steps

1 Open the Drawing toolbar from the View > Toolbars menu or click on the Drawing button 🐾.

2 Select a free line, rectangle, oval or other AutoShape from the toolbar then move the pointer on the screen. It will show a cross.

3 Click and drag the cross across the page to create the shape.

4 Double-click the mouse to stop drawing curves or free shapes.

When you want to add arrows, squares or freestyle drawings of your own, you can use the range of drawing tools available within Word.

Once you have drawn a basic shape, you can fill it with colour, rotate or flip it or select several shapes and group them into one.

Apart from the more commonly used lines, arrows and geometric shapes, you can add Callouts as 'speech bubbles', or WordArt text in bendy shapes. You can also box text and make it stand out with colours, shadows or 3-D effects.

AutoShapes · Drawing Toolbar · ClipArt · Fill Color · Line Color · Text box · Box styles · Drawing shapes · Line and arrow styles

Grouping · Reorder objects

Tip

The Drawing Canvas normally appears automatically. If you do not want this, go to Tools > Options and deselect the option on the General tab.

Using some of the Drawing tools

Simple drawing

3-D effect

Shadow

Resized callout

Rotated Autoshape

Fill Effects – texture

Fill Effects – patterns

❑ Editing a shape

1 Click to show the white sizing handles.

2 Drag any sizing handle with the 2-way arrow to increase or decrease the size of the shape. On a callout, you can drag a yellow triangle appearing at its tip to change its position on the marked object.

3 When the mouse pointer shows a 4-way arrow, click on the drawn object to drag it around the screen.

4 Change the line style or fill colour using the toolbar options.

5 To rotate a shape, click on it then drag the green circle to turn it around its centre.

Tip

To box text, either draw a **Text Box** first, entering text where the cursor is flashing, or draw a rectangle round entries. You may need to select **Draw > Order > Send Behind Text**, or use **Fill > No Fill,** to reveal the text underneath.

Borders and shading

1 Select the text and go to Format > Borders and Shading...

2 On the Borders tab, select the type of border, the line thickness (width) and style, and check that these are applied to the correct section.

❑ To remove the border select *None* as the Setting.

3 On the Shading tab you can add coloured or patterned backgrounds to the box.

4 Select Page Border to edge the page with lines or pictures.

5 Click OK to return to your document.

You can create attractive boxes of text by bordering and shading parts of a document, and you can also border a whole page. The options are in the **Format > Borders and Shading** dialog box.

When text borders appear, they often apply to the entire paragraph. Select the text and then click Apply to Text if you want the border to fit just the text entry.

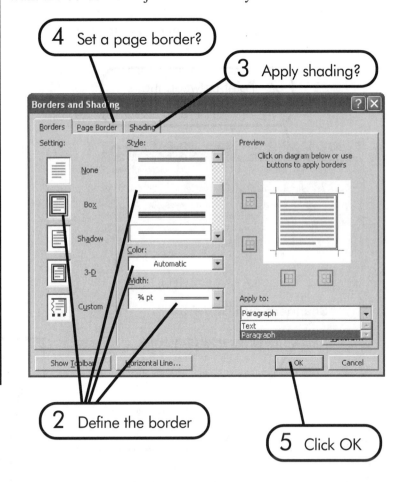

4 Set a page border?

3 Apply shading?

2 Define the border

5 Click OK

Margins

Every new document has a left, right, top and bottom margin where text is not normally typed. The default settings are:

Top and Bottom 1" (2.54 cm)

Left and Right 1.5" (3.17 cm)

For some documents, these white spaces may be too wide or too narrow and you will want to change them. You can either change the measurements exactly, or do it roughly by eye using the Ruler.

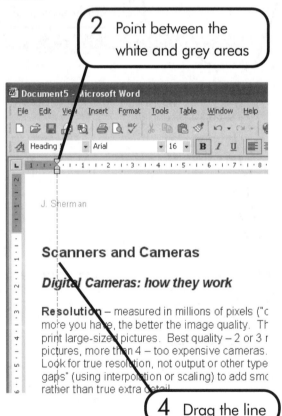

2 Point between the white and grey areas

4 Drag the line

- Using the Ruler

1 Select View > Print Layout to show the margins clearly.

2 Move the mouse pointer between the white and grey areas on the ruler until it changes to a two-way arrow.

3 Click and hold the button and a dotted line will appear down the page.

4 Drag the line in the appropriate direction to increase or decrease the margin.

Take note

Measurements are normally shown in centimetres. To change the units, select **Tools > Options**, click the **General** tab and change the setting in the **Measurement units** box.

Basic steps

1 In the File > Page Set up dialog box, click the Margins tab.

2 For any margin, move the measurement up or down in 10ths by clicking the arrow.

Or

3 Type in new measurements – you do not need to add the units.

4 Set the Apply to option – the whole document, the section or from the current point forward.

5 If you want to use the new measurements regularly, click Default to set them for all new documents.

6 Preview the changes before clicking OK.

Using the dialog box

To alter margins exactly, click the Margin tab in the **File > Page Set up** dialog box and then change the measurements showing in the relevant boxes. Unlike paragraph formatting, you don't need to select any part of the document first unless you want the margin change restricted.

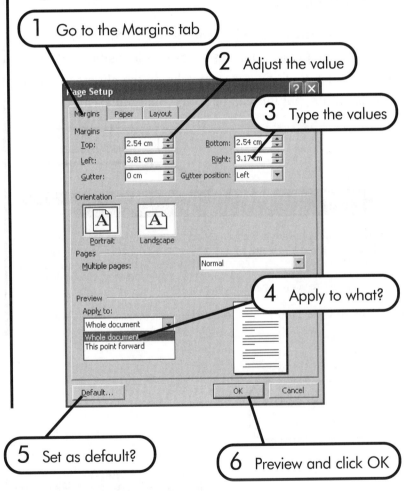

1 Go to the Margins tab

2 Adjust the value

3 Type the values

4 Apply to what?

5 Set as default?

6 Preview and click OK

Moving and copying text

It often happens that words, paragraphs or other items such as pictures need to be moved or copied to a different part of the document. To save retyping, you can use two different techniques commonly known as *drag and drop* and *cut and paste*.

Drag and drop

Dragging selected text with the mouse is best for moving single words or paragraphs short distances on the visible part of the screen. After dragging, text may take on the alignment of the closest entries, but this can be sorted out quite easily.

1 Select the text

Macro Mode – this allows you to focus closely. The smaller the figure, the better e.g. at 2cm a pound coin will almost fill the entire picture.

Memory – most have removable memory cards which can store between 10 – 20 shots each, and you are sure to need to buy an extra one as those supplied are usually small. There are different formats e.g. Compact Flash, Memory Sticks, Smart Media, XD cards etc. You need at least a 64Mb card which would cost around £40.

Flash – for better pictures, look for a camera with mounting for an extra flash gun

3 Drag across the screen

Memory – most have removable memory cards which can store between 10 – 20 shots each, and you are sure to need to buy an extra one as those supplied are usually small. There are different formats e.g. Compact Flash, Memory Sticks, Smart Media, XD cards etc. You need at least a 64Mb card which would cost around £40.
Macro Mode – this allows you to focus closely. The smaller the figure, the better e.g. at 2cm a pound coin will almost fill the entire picture.

Flash – for better pictures, look for a camera with mounting for an extra flash gun

4 Drop into place

Basic steps

1 Select the text.

2 Move the pointer over the block until it shows a white arrow. Hold down the button. A small box will appear at the end of the arrow.

3 Drag the arrow to the new position for the text. A vertical dotted line will move with it.

4 Release the mouse button and the text will drop into place.

☐ To copy, but not move, the text, hold down [Control] as you drag. A cross will appear below the box.

Basic steps

1 Select the text.

2 Use a toolbar button, or select the Edit menu, or right-click on the text and pick from the short menu: Cut ✂ to move, Copy ▣ for a copy.

3 Click in the new position for the text.

4 Click Paste ▣ or Select Edit – Paste.

5 Click an option on the Paste button.

Cut and Paste

To move larger blocks of text over longer distances, perhaps across pages or to another document or application altogether, it is best to use Cut/Copy and Paste.

To leave the original in place, a **copy** of the selected text is placed in a temporary part of the computer's memory known as the Clipboard. To move text, you must **cut** it out of the document before placing it in the Clipboard. When ready, text from the Clipboard is **pasted** into its new position.

By default, formatting is copied along with the text. You can control this with the options on the button which appears after pasting.

Tip

Things can go wrong, so if working with painstakingly constructed text or images, copy rather than cut before pasting. This way, the original cannot be lost in transit.

The Clipboard in Word

Earlier versions of Word only allowed one item at a time to be held in the Clipboard, but now it can store up to 24 different entries at once. This means that you can transfer a number of entries across pages, documents or even applications.

1 Cut or copy items as normal.

2 If you want to paste the last item cut or copied, then Paste as normal.

3 If you have cut or copied more than one item, the Clipboard should open in the Task Pane automatically. If it does not, show it by selecting Edit > Office Clipboard. Each item will be listed.

4 Click an item or select Paste to insert it at the current place in your document.

5 To empty the Clipboard click Clear All.

6 To paste all the items at once click Paste All.

6 Paste all items at once

5 Empty the Clipboard

4 Click to paste an item

Find or replace text

□ To replace text

1 Select Edit > Replace.

2 Enter the original text in the Find What box *exactly* as it appears in the document.

3 Enter the new text in the Replace With box.

4 Click Find Next. The first matching text will be highlighted in your document.

5 Click Replace, or Find Next to skip to the next match.

□ To find text

6 Select Edit > Find or click 🔍 and complete the boxes as above.

7 Click Find Next to locate the first matching entry.

A useful shortcut offered by Word when working with longer documents is to find and replace text or punctuation automatically, or go directly to a particular page. You could, for example, use an abbreviation throughout a document and replace all such entries with the full text that only needs to be typed once, or find a reference to a particular word without searching every page.

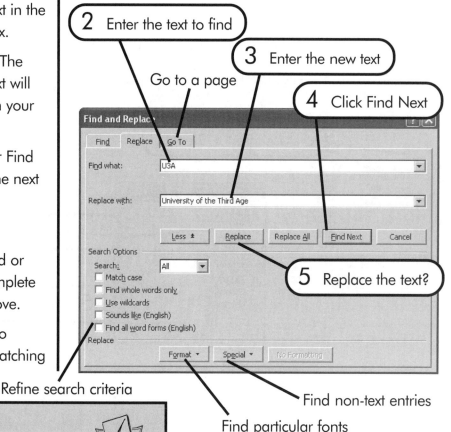

2 Enter the text to find

3 Enter the new text

Go to a page

4 Click Find Next

5 Replace the text?

Refine search criteria

Find particular fonts or other features

Find non-text entries

Starting a new page

As you type a long document, a new page starts automatically when you reach the bottom of the screen. However, the page breaks may change later as you add or delete text or images.

If you always want an entry to start on a new page, perhaps a fresh chapter or the first piece of text following a title page, you need to produce a 'hard break' in your document. This will then be retained whatever happens to the rest of your work.

To see the break, click ¶ the Show/Hide button that reveals all keyboard strokes and you will see it represented as follows:

.....................................Page Break.......................................

1 Click the cursor in the position for the break.

2 Use the keyboard shortcut: [Control] plus [Enter].

Or

3 Open the Insert menu and select Break...

4 Check the Page break option is selected.

5 Click OK.

6 To delete the break, click on the dotted line and press [Delete].

3 Use Insert > Break...

Insert
- Break...
- Page Numbers...
- Date and Time...
- Symbol...
- Picture ▶
- Hyperlink... Ctrl+K

Break [?][X]

Break types
- ● Page break
- ○ Column break
- ○ Text wrapping break

Section break types
- ○ Next page
- ○ Continuous
- ○ Even page
- ○ Odd page

OK   Cancel

4 Select Page break

5 Click OK

Tip

You can sometimes create unwanted page breaks by accident, which will spread your document over several blank pages. To delete these, move to the end page and click the Show/Hide button. Now delete all the Enter symbols ¶ until you find yourself back on the last page of text.

Basic steps

1 Select Insert – Page Numbers to open the dialog box.

2 Choose where the numbers should go.

3 Click Format...

4 If required, change the style (e.g. i, ii, iii, etc.) or start numbering other than from page 1 and click OK.

5 Check the preview and click OK.

You can choose to omit numbers on the first page of a document

Page numbers

Rather than number each page manually, which would mean amending numbers as you add extra pages of typing, Word will insert page numbers into the top or bottom margin and update them automatically.

You can include page numbers within a header or footer (see page 61) or insert them from the **Insert** menu.

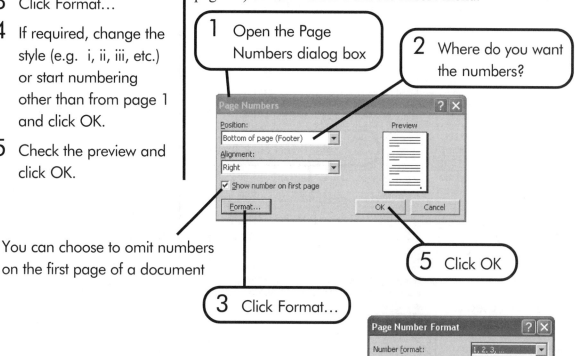

1 Open the Page Numbers dialog box

2 Where do you want the numbers?

Page Numbers

Position:
Bottom of page (Footer)

Alignment:
Right

☑ Show number on first page

Format...

Preview

OK   Cancel

5 Click OK

3 Click Format...

Page Number Format

Number format: 1, 2, 3, ...

☐ Include chapter number

Chapter starts with style   Heading 1

Use separator: - (hyphen)

Examples: 1-1, 1-A

Page numbering
○ Continue from previous section
○ Start at:

OK   Cancel

4 Set the style and start

Take note

Page numbers are not visible in Normal view. Select **View > Print Layout** or preview your document by going to **File > Print Preview** to check that they are in the correct place.

Symbols and dates

To enter a character not available on the keyboard, you can select a symbol from the range available in the Symbol box. You can also save time entering the date by selecting it from the **Insert** menu.

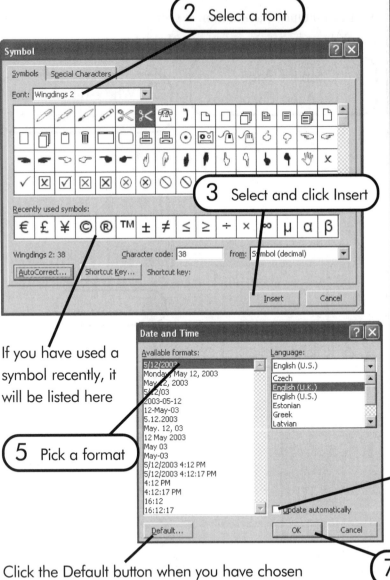

2 Select a font

3 Select and click Insert

If you have used a symbol recently, it will be listed here

5 Pick a format

6 Update?

7 Click OK

Click the Default button when you have chosen your preferred style of date or time. It will then be selected whenever you open the dialog box.

Basic steps

❑ Inserting symbols

1 Click in position for the symbol in your document, and then go to Insert > Symbol.

2 Scroll through the fonts to view the sets.

3 Select a symbol, click Insert then click Close.

❑ Inserting the date

4 Select Insert > Date and Time.

5 Select your preferred format and click OK.

6 If you will be delaying printing but want the current date in your document, select Update automatically.

7 Click OK.

Basic steps

- ❑ Previously saved object

1 Select Insert – Object and click the Create from File tab.

2 In the dialog box, type in the file name, or click Browse to locate the file – the name will be inserted into the File name box.

3 If you click Link to file, changes made to the original will be reflected in the Word document.

4 Select Display as icon if you want to save space.

5 Click OK to import the file into your document.

6 Double-click the object to go to the original application for editing.

- ❑ Handwriting

7 If handwriting recognition is installed, you can write with the mouse to insert text.

You can use any of the applications on your computer to create objects such as charts, 'post-it' notes or pictures within your document, or locate and import one that was previously created elsewhere. You can even use your mouse to add text directly.

When you double-click the imported object, you can use the toolbars and menu options available in the original application to make any changes.

You can also choose to insert just an icon representing the object, which you must then double-click to view.

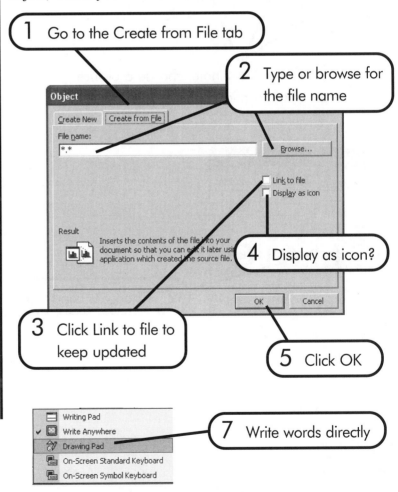

1 Go to the Create from File tab

2 Type or browse for the file name

4 Display as icon?

3 Click Link to file to keep updated

5 Click OK

7 Write words directly

4 Create the object

To create a Post-It note, choose a picture,
then type a caption and the note

7 Choose a chart type

❑ New object

1 Select Insert > Object
and click the Create
New tab.

2 Scroll down until you
find a suitable object.

3 Select it and click OK.

4 Use the toolbars and
menus that appear to
create the object.

5 Click *outside* the object
or click OK to return to
your Word document.

6 Double-click the object
for editing.

7 For diagrams, click the
Insert Diagram button
on the Drawing
toolbar, then select a
diagram style at the
Gallery.

Basic steps

1 Select View > Headers and Footers .

2 For a header, enter your text in the box, formatting it as normal. Press [Tab] to move across the box to centre or right-align an entry.

3 Use the toolbar to insert page numbers, dates or times.

4 To set different headers within a document, go to Page Set up > Layout.

5 To go to the footer box, click the Switch Between Header and Footer button.

6 Close the toolbar and check in Print Layout view (where header text is shown in grey).

7 To delete headers or footers, double-click the entry or select View > Headers and Footers and switch to the relevant box. Ensure text is fully selected before pressing [Delete].

If you want the same text at the top or bottom of every page, e.g. a company logo or the title of your report, you can insert entries in the margins as headers or footers. This way, they don't affect the layout of your work and you can even have different entries on the front or alternate pages.

When you are creating headers or footers, the text of your document is shown in grey. Switch between views by double-clicking the text in the header box or in your main document.

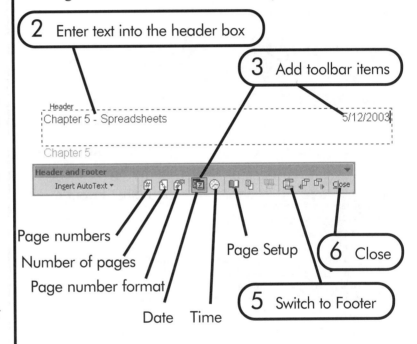

2 Enter text into the header box

3 Add toolbar items

Header
Chapter 5 - Spreadsheets   5/12/2003

Chapter 5

Header and Footer
Insert AutoText ▾

Page numbers
Number of pages
Page number format
Date   Time
Page Setup
6 Close
5 Switch to Footer

Take note

Page numbers, dates or times inserted from the Header and Footer toolbar are updated automatically.

Creating lists

Whenever you have a list of entries that need to be numbered, you can either set numbering before you type, or add the numbers later. In the same way, you can emphasise points with bullets. Once numbers or bullets have been set, they are added automatically when you press **[Enter]** and start a new line.

1 Click the ⊞ Bullets or ⊞ Numbers toolbar button. A number or bullet will appear at the beginning of the line.

2 After your first item, press [Enter] to start the next line with a bullet or number.

3 Complete your list, press [Enter] and turn off the toolbar button.

4 To create a line in the middle of the list *without* numbers or bullets, hold [Shift] as you press [Enter] or select it later and turn off the button.

5 To add or amend bullets or numbers *after* completing a list, select all the entries and click the toolbar button.

1 Click Bullets or Numbers

3 Click to turn off again

Click to show or hide the paragraph, tab and other layout marks

2 Press [Enter] at the end of the line

4 Hold [Shift] for an unnumbered line

Take note

If you click the **Show/Hide** button ¶, you will see the symbol at the end of the line looks different.

Formatting bullets and numbers

1 To change number or bullet attributes, open the Format > Bullets and Numbering dialog box.

2 Select the appropriate tab.

3 Click on a style.

4 If you break off a list, e.g. to insert a drawing, select the Restart or Continue option if necessary.

5 Click OK.

❑ Customising

6 To customise styles, or alter the spacing between numbers or bullets and list items, click Customize...

7 Define the style and click OK.

The toolbar buttons are easy to use, but go to the **Format – Bullets and Numbering** menu to amend styles or spacing.

Tables

To create neat columns of text or numbers in your work, you can insert a table and enter your data into the boxes – *cells* – that appear. Each cell is independent and so entries can be aligned or formatted differently within each one.

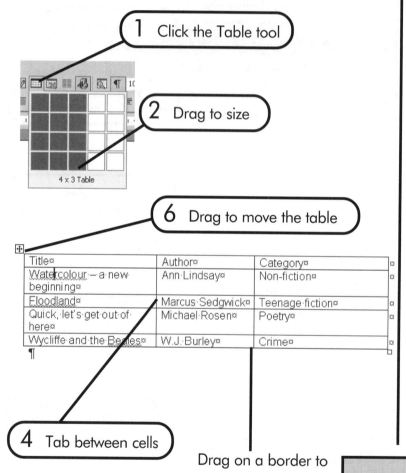

1 Click the Table tool

2 Drag to size

4 x 3 Table

6 Drag to move the table

Title¤	Author¤	Category¤	¤
Watercolour – a new beginning¤	Ann·Lindsay¤	Non-fiction¤	¤
Floodland¤	Marcus·Sedgwick¤	Teenage·fiction¤	¤
Quick,·let's·get·out·of·here¤	Michael·Rosen¤	Poetry¤	¤
Wycliffe·and·the·Beatles¤	W.J.·Burley¤	Crime¤	¤

4 Tab between cells

Drag on a border to alter the table size

1 Position the cursor then click the Table tool.

2 Drag the mouse across the required number of cells and, when you let go a table will appear.

Or

3 Select Table > Insert Table, enter the number of rows and columns in the dialog box and click OK.

4 Use [Tab] or the mouse to move between cells for text entry.

5 Press [Enter] to create a new line within the cell, or let word wrap fill the cell with a long entry.

6 To move the table, click and drag the small selection box.

Take note

Selecting cells and pressing [Delete] will only remove cell entries and will NOT remove entire columns or rows.

Basic steps

☐ Inserting and deleting

1 Click in the last cell and press [Tab] to add a new row.

Or

2 Select any cell and add a column or row by going to Table > Insert and choosing a Row or Column option.

3 To delete a column or row, select it then use Table > Delete and click a delete option.

☐ Enhancing

4 Format selected cells or the table via the Borders and Shading dialog box (page 49).

5 To remove borders, set Settings to *None*.

Or

6 For colours or shading use the borders and backgrounds options on the Tables and Borders toolbar.

Amending columns and rows

You will probably find that you need to change the width or height of your table to accommodate entries, and add or delete extra rows or columns once you start entering your data.

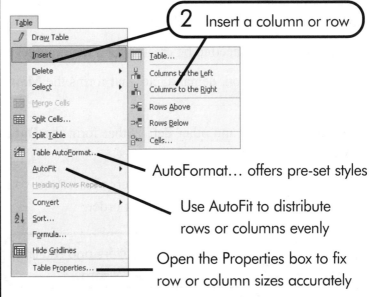

2 Insert a column or row

AutoFormat... offers pre-set styles

Use AutoFit to distribute rows or columns evenly

Open the Properties box to fix row or column sizes accurately

Improving the appearance of a table

Cell borders can be removed before printing to leave simple columns, or retained and emphasised to print data out as a grid.

6 Use the toolbar

Draw a table manually
Line style
Border colour
Shading colour
Select borders to format

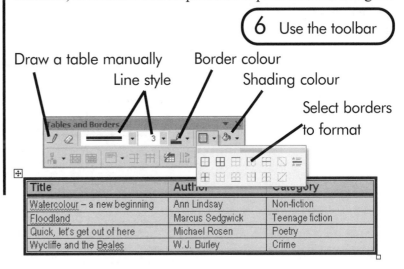

Title	Author	Category
Watercolour – a new beginning	Ann Lindsay	Non-fiction
Floodland	Marcus Sedgwick	Teenage fiction
Quick, let's get out of here	Michael Rosen	Poetry
Wycliffe and the Beales	W. J. Burley	Crime

Mail merge

It is always pleasanter to receive a personalised letter or invitation than one addressed to 'Dear Sir/Madam'. In order to save time when sending out such documents, you can build up a database of details for everyone on your mailing list and add the appropriate information to each letter automatically.

There are two files that need to be created for a mail merge:

● The letter, invitation, demand, etc. that forms the **Main Document**;

● Names, addresses and other details that form the **Data Source**.

By following the steps set out in the Mail Merge Task Pane, you can create and edit your files in the correct order.

❑ Create Main Document

1 Wherever you are in Word, select Tools > Letters and Mailings > Mail Merge Wizard.

2 In Step 1 select Letters for everything apart from e-mails, labels and envelopes. Click Next.

3 At Step 2, select a new or existing document. Click Next.

The next job is to create the mailing list.

1 Use Tools > Letters and Mailings > Mail merge Wizard...

3 Select Letters

Basic steps

1 To create a mailing list, click Type a new list and then click Create.

2 Complete the details for the first person on your list and then click New Entry.

3 If you want to change the fields, click Customize…

4 Select any unwanted field and click Delete, or add new ones.

5 Click OK to return to the New Address List dialog box.

6 Move between your records by clicking Previous or Next.

7 When all names have been added, click Close and save the Data Source file.

8 You will be offered the chance to sort or filter your list, or you can add or amend names by clicking Edit recipient list in the Task Pane.

Creating the mailing list

You will now be offered a standard list of categories (or *fields*) for your mailing list e.g. first name, surname, town, etc. After amending the field names, use the Address List box to enter details of everyone on your mailing list.

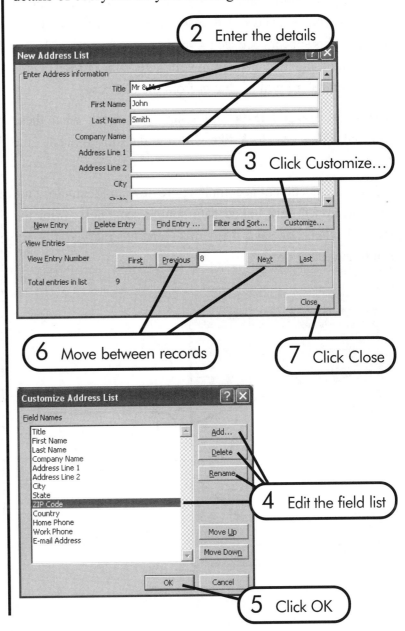

2 Enter the details

3 Click Customize…

6 Move between records

7 Click Close

4 Edit the field list

5 Click OK

When you have entered all the records into your database, you'll return to your Main Document where a new toolbar appears – the Mail Merge toolbar.

Now you can start completing your Main Document. Don't type everyone's details, but insert the relevant field name instead. This appears between <<chevrons>> against a shaded background and, when you print your letters, the correct details from each record will be drawn from the database.

The **View Merged Data** button lets you check what these finished letters will look like with the data inserted into the fields.

When your document is complete, preview and then close the main document and linked data source separately, print the merged letters, or save them in a separate merged file for printing another day.

1 Select a field and click Insert

1 Create a document as normal but instead of typing the name or other details, e.g. after *Dear,* insert a field name from the Insert Merge Field box.

2 Continue typing and inserting field names until your document is complete.

3 Click the View Merged Data button to see the first record or return to the Main Document.

4 Click the Next Record button to see the next.

5 Click Merge to New Document to save the merged documents in a separate file.

6 Click Merge to Printer to print the documents.

7 Save and close the Main Document and the Data Source file.

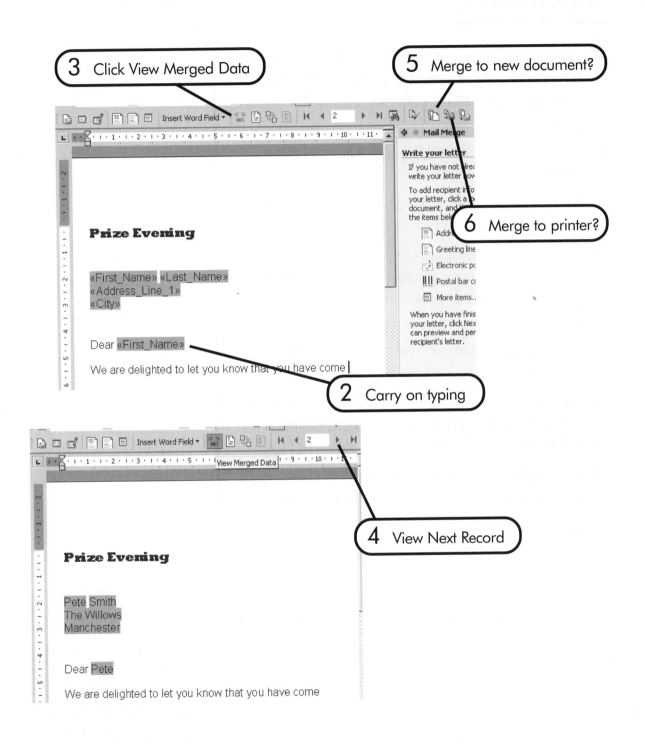

3 Click View Merged Data

5 Merge to new document?

6 Merge to printer?

Mail Merge

Write your letter

If you have not alrea
write your letter now

To add recipient info
your letter, click a lo
document, and
the items belo

Addr

Greeting line

Electronic po

Postal bar co

More items..

When you have finis
your letter, click Nex
can preview and per
recipient's letter.

Prize Evening

«First_Name» «Last_Name»
«Address_Line_1»
«City»

Dear «First_Name»

We are delighted to let you know that you have come

2 Carry on typing

4 View Next Record

View Merged Data

Prize Evening

Pete Smith
The Willows
Manchester

Dear Pete

We are delighted to let you know that you have come

Summary

❑ Your own drawings, or pictures from the Gallery, can be inserted into documents and then moved, re-sized or otherwise altered using the editing and formatting tools.

❑ Another way to enhance text is to add a border or shade the background.

❑ Margins can be altered by eye or by an exact figure entered in the margin measurement boxes.

❑ When you want to copy or re-position any entries, you can drag them to new places or copy them over and over again using the Paste option.

❑ If you need a special symbol, or a chart or drawing produced elsewhere, you can add or link it to your document.

❑ You can also add page numbers and dates that will update automatically over time, and include the same entries on every page by creating headers or footers.

❑ Lists can be numbered or enhanced with bullets, and the style and spacing can be customised to your liking.

❑ You can insert tables to present information in a grid format.

❑ To save time sending the same letter to a number of people, you can type it once and then personalise it by merging it with data held in a separately created database.

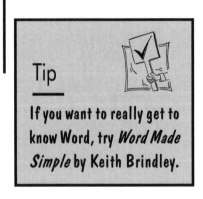

Tip

If you want to really get to know Word, try *Word Made Simple* by Keith Brindley.

5 Spreadsheets

The right address

Moving around

Spreadsheets allow you to present numerical data and perform calculations. They can be particularly useful at home if you want to keep an eye on your finances, work out quantities for DIY or cooking, keep scores in games or compare prices.

When you open Microsoft Excel from the icon ▣ or the **Start > All Programs** menu, the first sheet of your workbook opens directly on screen. You can make entries on any sheet by clicking the sheet tab at the bottom of the screen, and all sheets will be saved automatically when you save the file.

Each sheet looks like squared paper and each square is known as a *cell*. At the head of each column of cells is a letter, and there is a number at the start of each row. So that you can refer to a particular cell on the sheet, each cell is known by its column and row e.g. A2 or B3. This is the *cell address*.

❑ To go to a cell, use any of these methods:

Click into the cell

Press [Tab] to move a column to the right

Hold [Shift] as you press [Tab] to move to the left

Press [Enter] to move down the column

Press an arrow key to move in that direction

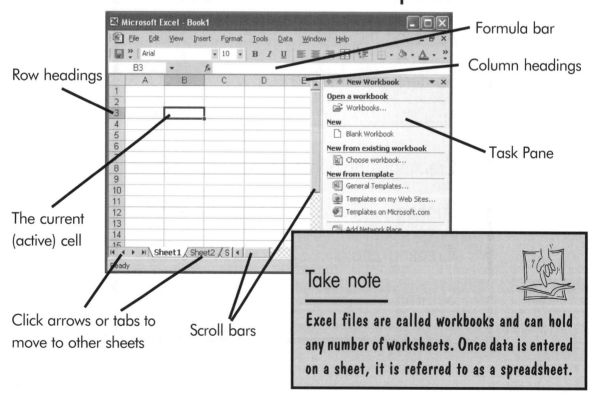

Formula bar

Column headings

Row headings

Task Pane

The current (active) cell

Click arrows or tabs to move to other sheets

Scroll bars

Take note

Excel files are called workbooks and can hold any number of worksheets. Once data is entered on a sheet, it is referred to as a spreadsheet.

Basic steps

- ❑ Selecting cells

1 Click or move to any cell. It will show a darker border and is known as the active cell. (A1 is automatically selected at first.)

2 To select more than one cell at a time, move the pointer over the first cell in the range. It will show a fat white cross .

3 Click and drag the cross down the column or along the row. Adjacent cells will now all be selected.

4 After making changes to the selected cells, click anywhere on the sheet to remove the highlight.

5 To select non-adjacent rows or columns, select the first block of cells, then hold down [Control] as you select further blocks.

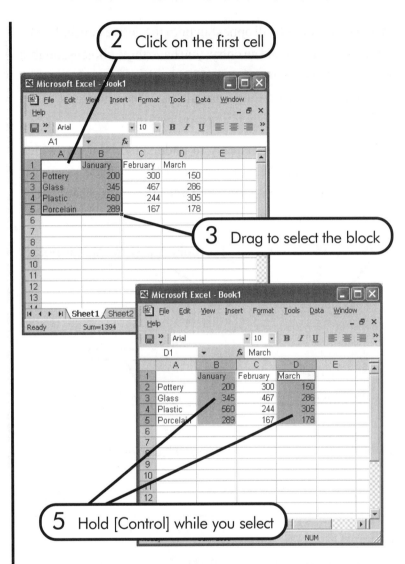

2 Click on the first cell

3 Drag to select the block

5 Hold [Control] while you select

Take note

When selecting cells, the first cell remains white but is still selected along with the others in the range.

Creating a spreadsheet

As you type, entries will appear in both the active cell and in the Formula bar. To amend an entry, you have three choices: double click the cell; select it and press [F2] to place the cursor inside; or click on the entry in the Formula bar. Then delete or insert entries as you would when word-processing.

So that the spreadsheet is easy to understand, you can widen columns, re-format headings and border or shade particular sections. You can then print the results as a spreadsheet or use the data to create a chart.

Basic steps

1 Open Excel and move to the first cell for data entry.

2 Enter text, symbols or numbers into the active cell.

3 Move down columns or across rows to enter data in different cells.

4 Amend cell entries if you make a mistake or want to reformat entries – full details on the following pages.

5 Save the workbook by clicking the Save button and entering its name and location in the Save As dialog box.

Address of active cell

Formula bar showing formula

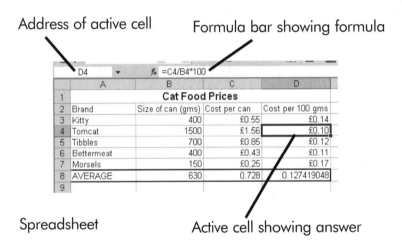

Spreadsheet

Active cell showing answer

Chart

Basic steps

1 Click in the cell where you want the answer to appear.

2 Type the formula, starting with '=' and using operators, cell addresses and values.

3 Press [Enter] or click the ✓ on the Formula bar.

4 Check that the answer is as expected.

5 If it looks incorrect, check your formula in the Formula bar and correct as necessary.

Tip

Instead of *typing* a cell address, you can click on it and its address will be entered into your formula.

Arithmetic operators

+ add	- subtract
* multiply	/divide
^ to the power of	% percentage

Calculations

The joy of Excel is that it will perform calculations for you – but you do have to give it the right instructions. To add the numbers in column A and put a total in A4, you need to write the correct formula. This can use the actual numbers, or the cell addresses.

● For any formula you first enter = to tell Excel to perform a calculation.

● You could now enter the numbers and operators
e.g. =15+14+18

● Use addresses, rather than numbers, so that if you alter the cell contents later, the total is updated automatically
e.g. =A1+A2+A3

This is because the instruction is 'add the contents A1, A2 and A3'. If the contents change, the total will change.

1 Click into the cell

2 Type the formula

4 Check the answer

Useful formulae

For simple calculations, you can use actual figures or cell addresses and simply enter the correct data and operators before pressing [Enter]

$$= A15/7.5$$

When a large number of cells are involved, it can be tedious to enter all the details into a formula. Instead, you can make use of one of the automatic *functions* available in Excel that offer pre-defined formulae structured to perform calculations.

Of the many available functions, you are most likely to use SUM to total the contents of a range of cells, and AVERAGE to calculate averages. There is a shortcut to the Sum function – the AutoSum. Other commonly-used functions can be selected from the drop-down list on the AutoSum button. For the full range of functions, open the Insert Function dialog box by clicking the f_x button on the Formula Bar.

☐ To use a function

1 Type the = sign then the name of the function (upper or lower case) and an opening bracket e.g. =SUM(

2 Enter the cell range by typing the first cell, then a colon and then the last cell e.g. B2:B6

Or

3 Click the first cell and drag down to the last to enter the range into the formula.

4 Press [Enter] – there is no need to enter the closing bracket first.

☐ AutoSum

5 Select the range of cells.

6 Click the AutoSum button Σ ▾.

The total will appear in the next available cell

1 Start the function

2 Enter the cell range

6 Click AutoSum

3 Select the range of cells

Formatting text

Basic steps

1 Select the cell(s) you want to change.

2 Click the appropriate toolbar shortcut or go to Format > Cells.

3 Select the Font tab to change the text style, type or size.

4 Preview the changes and then click OK.

Once you have entered text into a cell, you can make various changes to its appearance. Here are some examples:

Regular text (left aligned in cell)
Bold text
Italic text
<u>Underlined text</u>
Right aligned text
Centred text
DIFFERENT FONT TYPE
Different font size

Formatting toolbar

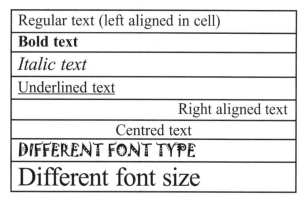

Font · Size · Alignment · Merge and Center Cells · Bold · Italic · Underline

Format dialog box, Font tab

Click to change orientation or alignment

Take note

If you find you can't click on a menu option, it could mean your cursor is still in the cell. Click or tab away and then select the cell again. You should now be able to carry out your formatting.

Improving headings

You can improve the appearance of header text in two different ways. Centre a heading with the Merge cells facility, or keep columns narrow by 'wrapping' the heading text.

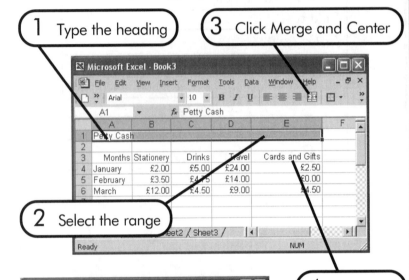

1 Type the heading

3 Click Merge and Center

2 Select the range

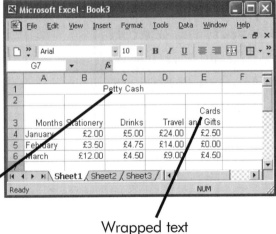

You can Merge Cells from here

Merged and centred

Wrapped text

❑ Centre a heading

1 Type the heading text in the first cell, e.g. A1.

2 Select the range of cells across the width of your data, e.g. A1:E1.

3 Click the Merge and Center toolbar button.

❑ Using wrap text

4 Type the heading.

5 Select Format > Cells and click the Alignment tab.

6 Select Wrap text and click OK.

7 If necessary, increase the row height to accommodate the text.

4 Enter the heading

6 Select Wrap text

Basic steps

1 Select the cell(s) to be formatted.

2 Click the appropriate toolbar button.

Or

3 Use Format>Cells and go to the Number tab.

4 Select the Category, and amend the Decimal places or Symbol if relevant.

5 Check the sample to make sure formatting is correct and click OK.

❑ To retain numbers starting with 0, e.g. telephone or stock code numbers, format as *Text* or type an apostrophe before the number e.g. '020 7...

Tip

If you find '$' inserted instead of '£', go to **Format > Style > Modify** and select the UK symbol from the list.

Numbers

You can change what you see on screen without changing the underlying *value* of any numeric entry made into a cell by formatting the numbers.

The default setting is *General* so that the cell will display the exact entry. Alternative ways to show the same number, e.g. 7.66 include:

8	*Number* with no decimals, i.e. Integer
7.7	*Number* with one decimal place
£7.66	*Currency* with two decimal places
7.66%	*Percentage* with two decimal places

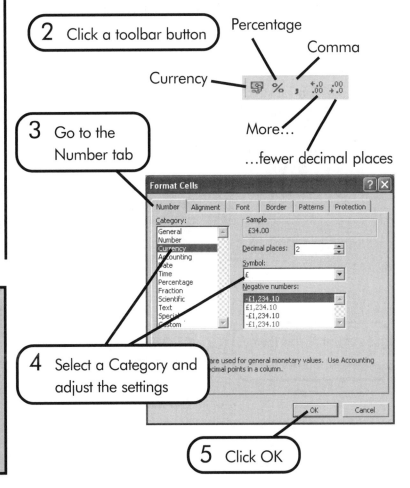

2 Click a toolbar button

Percentage

Comma

Currency

More...

...fewer decimal places

3 Go to the Number tab

4 Select a Category and adjust the settings

5 Click OK

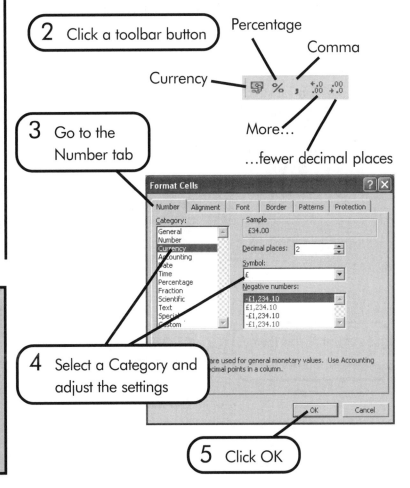

79

Copying formulae

Many spreadsheets need you to repeat the same calculation across a number of columns or rows, e.g. totals for monthly expenditure, average rainfall over years, final exam results for 30 different children, etc.

Excel takes out the tedium by allowing you to copy formulae to other cells accurately. It uses *relative cell references*, i.e. the relative positions of the cells.

In the example below, the instruction in B8 can be translated as 'sum the contents of the four cells *above* the active cell' which results in the addition of the contents of B4, B5, B6 and B7. If this instruction is then copied to C8, it will result in the addition of the contents of C4, C5, C6 and C7.

□ Using the mouse

1 Enter the formula or data into the first cell.

2 Move the pointer over the black box in the bottom, right-hand corner of the cell (the fill handle) until it changes to a black cross.

3 Click and drag the cross in the direction for copying. Dotted lines will appear round the cells.

4 Let go and the totals or repeated entries will appear. Amend the formatting if necessary.

5 For copied formulae, click one new total to check that the formula refers to the appropriate column or row.

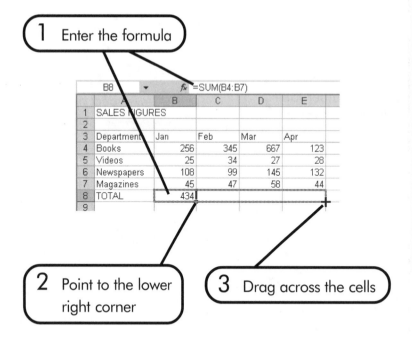

1 Enter the formula

2 Point to the lower right corner

3 Drag across the cells

Basic steps

❑ Using the menu

1 Enter the first formula or other data and then select this cell and all the cells in the range to take the copied entry.

2 Go to Edit > Fill and select the direction for copying, or Series to copy different types of entry in specific steps.

3 For Series, specify the Type, Step and Stop values as appropriate.

❑ You can also move or copy entries using Cut/ Copy and Paste, just as you do in word-processing, or you can drag selected entries to a new position when the mouse pointer shows an arrow. Hold down [Control] to copy rather than move the contents as you drag.

Fill Series

In most cases, copying text or numbers will fill all the selected cells with the same entry. However, if you enter a date e.g. January or Monday, copying will continue the date series automatically.

If you want to copy numbers by incremental steps, either enter *two* consecutive numbers and select both cells before copying from the second with the pointer, or use the **Edit > Fill > Series** option.

Tip

A quick way to copy data to a different cell is to type = and then the cell address of the original entry. Press [Enter] and a copy will appear. It will change if the original cell's contents are changed.

Absolute cell references

Where you don't want the contents of a particular cell in a formula to change during copying, e.g. if it contains a set percentage, unit of measurement or exchange rate etc., you have to 'fix' its position. In Excel, you do this by marking it with $ signs. You can then copy formulae to reflect changing rows or columns and the address of the cell you have marked remains *Absolute.*

1 Enter the formula in the first cell as normal.

2 Add $ signs automatically to the cell you wish to set as absolute by clicking between its address letter and number in the formula bar and pressing [F4].

Or

3 Type the $ signs in front of the letter and number of the cell you wish to fix as you enter its address into your formula.

4 Press [Enter] to accept the formula and then copy down or across in the usual way.

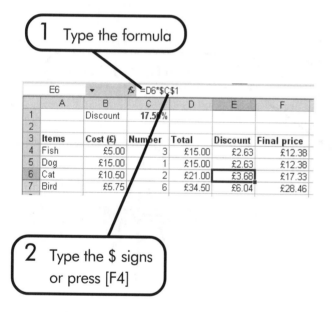

1 Type the formula

2 Type the $ signs or press [F4]

Take note

Take care to put $ signs in front of both letter and number of the cell address or the column or row will not be fixed.

Adjusting the grid

□ Inserting columns or rows

1 Click the column header to the *right* of the position for a new column. The complete column will be selected.

2 Select Insert > Column and a new column will slide into place.

3 Select more than one column to insert that number of new ones.

4 For a new row, select as many rows as you want to insert, *below* the new row position.

□ Deleting columns and rows

5 Select the column/row.

6 Open the Edit menu and select Delete.

If you want to insert new columns or rows into a spreadsheet, the letter or number headings are adjusted automatically and the new columns or rows appear to 'slide' into place. This adjustment also occurs if you delete columns or rows.

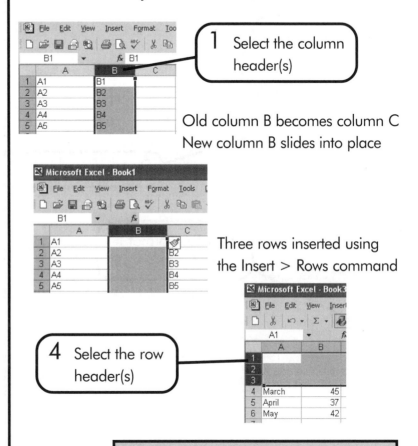

1 Select the column header(s)

Old column B becomes column C
New column B slides into place

Three rows inserted using the Insert > Rows command

4 Select the row header(s)

Tip

When deleting, don't just select cells and press **[Delete]**. If you do, only the cell *contents* will disappear and the column or row headings will not be adjusted automatically.

Column and row sizes

Quite often you will find that the standard width of columns or height of rows is not right for displaying your data. It is very easy to change the measurements – either by dragging with the mouse or using the menus.

1 **Point between the headers**

2 **Drag to resize**

4 **Select Format > Column or Row**

Tip

If you see ### appear, it means the column is not wide enough to display the full entry. Just widen the column and the symbols will disappear.

1 To widen a column, move the pointer between its header and the one to its right.

2 When it shows a 2-way arrow, click and drag the edge of the box to the right. If it is too wide, drag to the left.

3 For rows, drag the lower edge of the row-header up or down with the 2-way arrow.

Or

4 Select the column or row, and use Format > Column/Row to open the dialog box.

5 Enter an exact measure into the Width/Height box.

Or

6 Select AutoFit so the column /row fits the widest/highest entry.

Or

7 Select Standard Width to return to the default measurement.

Borders and shading

Basic steps

1 Select the cells to be formatted.

2 Click the Border drop-down arrow and select an option to add boxes or single edge borders.

3 Go to Format > Cells > Border to choose new line styles and colours, and apply them to one or more borders.

4 Select a background colour from the Fill Colour palette on the toolbar, or a pattern from the Format > Cells > Patterns menu.

You can add borders or shading to individual cells, or apply these to all the data on a spreadsheet. Excel has a range of styles ready to select or customize via the **Format** > **AutoFormat** menu. You can also use the Borders and Fill Colour toolbar shortcuts or select a wider range of options from the **Format** > **Cells** > **Border** or **Patterns** menu tabs.

No borders

4 Set the Fill colour

2 Add a simple border

3 Open the Format Cells Border dialog box to define the border

Line style

Remove border

Partial borders

Preview effect

Add line colour

Tip

If you see a line in one cell that you cannot remove, it may be a border added by mistake. Just select the cell and click the Border option showing no lines.

Applying an AutoFormat

It may be easier to apply a ready-made design to your spreadsheet that includes borders, shading and font styles. There is a range of styles available in Excel and you can even customise the designs by limiting which formats to apply.

1 Select the spreadsheet cells and go to Format > AutoFormat.

2 Scroll down the examples until you find one you want to apply.

3 Click to clear any boxes in the Format to apply section to prevent that option being applied.

4 Click OK.

5 Back in your spreadsheet, use the Format menu to amend colours or fonts.

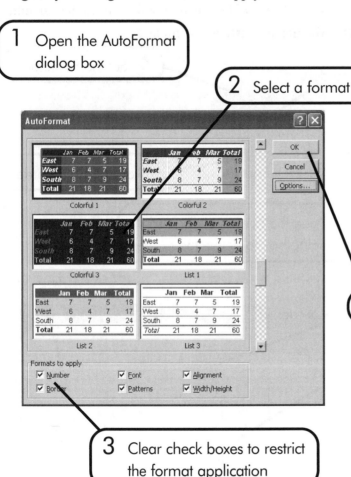

1 Open the AutoFormat dialog box

2 Select a format

4 Click OK

3 Clear check boxes to restrict the format application

Basic steps

1 Select View > Header/ Footer.

2 Select a Footer from the drop-down list.

Or

3 Click Custom Footer...

4 Click in the left, centre or right section to position the footer then enter text, or insert the date or page number.

5 To format text, select it and click the Font tool.

6 Click OK to return to the Page Setup to close or preview the footer or to create a header in the same way.

To add the date, your name or page numbers to your printouts, you can insert headers and footers. These are available from the **View** menu or the **File** > **Page Set up** dialog box and you can enter text directly, or insert options using the toolbar buttons.

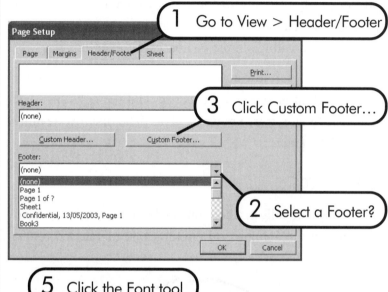

1 Go to View > Header/Footer

3 Click Custom Footer...

2 Select a Footer?

5 Click the Font tool

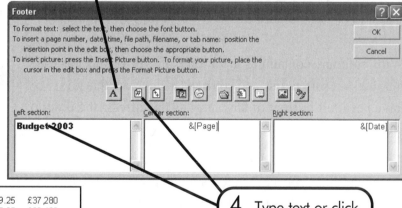

4 Type text or click a toolbar button

Footer showing on page

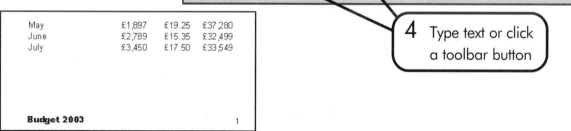

May	£1,897	£19.25	£37,280
June	£2,789	£15.35	£32,499
July	£3,450	£17.50	£33,549

Budget 2003   1

Creating a database

Databases are collections of items such as books, names and addresses, evening classes or houses for sale that are organised in a systematic way and can be sorted or searched. Unlike Microsoft Access, Excel is not a relational database application and doesn't have many of the complex facilities offered by purpose-built database software. However, it can be perfectly adequate for creating simple databases for everyday use.

In a database, each row containing data relating to one item in your collection is known as a *record*, and the columns under which data is stored are known as *fields*. The first row headings are the *field names*.

Sort records

The contents of cells in a column can be re-ordered very easily by selecting the column and clicking one of the AZ toolbar buttons.

Ascending – from a to z or lowest to highest number

Descending – from z to a or highest to lowest number

With columns containing a mixture of words and numbers, numbers are sorted first, and you need to take care that no spaces have been left in front of any entry as this affects the order of sort.

Although records in a database can be entered in any order on the spreadsheet, you may want to sort them so that they are listed in order of one field such as price, item or number in stock. If you select the complete range of cells and click an A–Z toolbar button, the sort will be based on the data in the first field on the left. If this is not the appropriate field, or you want different levels of sort, you need to use the **Data > Sort** menu.

Tip

If you want to create more sophisticated databases you need to use Microsoft Access. To find out more about this, read *Access Made Simple* by Moira Stephens.

Tip

Never select a single column in a database to sort or you will split up data relating to individual records and make nonsense of the information.

88

Basic steps

❑ Sorting a database

1 To sort on the first column, select the range of cells and click a Sort button.

Or

2 To sort on any other column, or to combine up to three levels of sort, select the cells and then go to Data > Sort.

3 Select the first column on which to base the sort from the list in the Sort by box, e.g. *Price*, in ascending order.

4 If necessary, add one or two further levels of sort, e.g. first by *Price*, then by *Item* and then by *Colour*.

5 If you selected field headings, click the *Header row* option under My list has, to remove the field names from the sort.

6 Click OK.

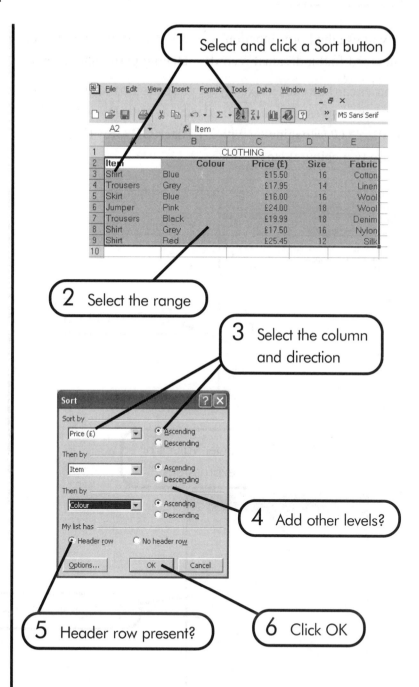

1 Select and click a Sort button

2 Select the range

3 Select the column and direction

4 Add other levels?

5 Header row present?

6 Click OK

Finding records

If you use the Form function, you can display one record at a time and find individual records matching particular criteria.

Entries can be matched exactly, or you can customise the search by using expressions in any field such as >20 (*Price* more than £20), Y* (*Item* beginning with Y), Black **OR** Grey (in either of these two colours) etc.

2 Click Criteria

3 Enter values or expressions

4 Click the Find buttons

❑ Using a form to find records

1 Select all the cells in the database.

2 Go to Data > Form and click the Criteria button.

3 In any of the empty field boxes, enter exact words or numbers, or your own expression, to find records matching the entry.

4 Click Find Previous or Find Next to work through the database locating matching records one at a time. For each record displayed, you will see which numbered record has been found.

Basic steps

1 Select the cells and go to Data > Filter > AutoFilter.

2 Each field name cell now has an arrow that you can click to drop down a list of all the entries in that field.

3 For any field, select the match from the list or click Custom …

4 In the Custom dialog box, select a logical operator, e.g. *is greater than, begins with*, etc. then enter your own data or select from the drop-down list in the right-hand pane.

5 Click OK and you will see a subset of the records in the database meeting this criterion.

6 Repeat with different criteria until you see just those records meeting all your criteria.

7 To return to the full database, select Data > Filter > Show All.

Filtering records

To display several records e.g. wool items under £15, or any blue shirts size 16, you can carry out a search using the AutoFilter command.

When filtering, the subset of records that is displayed can be printed or copied to a new location, or you can remove the filter and show all the records again.

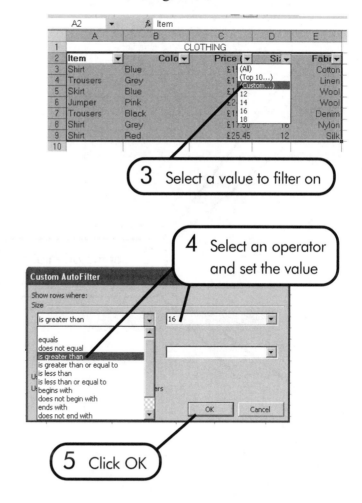

3 Select a value to filter on

4 Select an operator and set the value

5 Click OK

Printing

You can print spreadsheets with or without their gridlines, change to landscape orientation if some columns go over the page, or make sure you only print on one page by selecting *Fit to 1 page* to reduce the font size. All these options are available from the **File > Page Set up > Page** or **Sheet** menu.

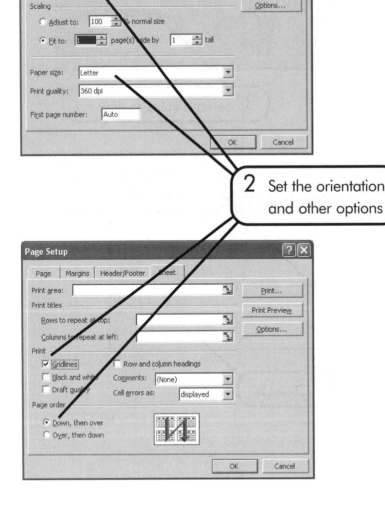

2 Set the orientation and other options

1 Check Print Preview, and if relevant go to Page Break Preview to alter the position for a page break.

2 Change orientation or make other changes using the File > Page Set up options.

3 For one copy of the data on the current sheet, click the Print toolbar button.

4 Go to File > Print to change to another printer, print several copies or print selected sheets.

Tip

When printing, you will print all rows and columns in which data has been entered. If you only want to print a small part of the spreadsheet, select the cells and then click *Selection* in the Print What box.

Basic steps

1 Select the data and its headings for the chart.

2 Click the Chart Wizard toolbar button.

3 Step 1: Select a chart type and preview its appearance before clicking Next.

4 Step 2: Select the data series – depending on whether you want row or column headings to form the X-axis labels, and if necessary, amend the Data range.

Creating charts

To display numerical information graphically, you can create a chart with the help of Excel's Chart Wizard. Choose from 2-D or 3-D column, bar, line, pie or less well-known chart types. You can add your own titles and either place the chart on its own sheet or 'float' it over your spreadsheet data.

The Chart Wizard makes columns or rows of values into separate data series that are named in the legend.

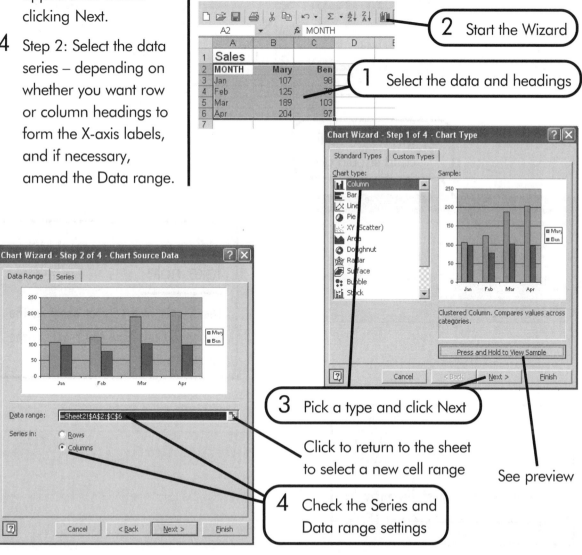

2 Start the Wizard

1 Select the data and headings

3 Pick a type and click Next

Click to return to the sheet to select a new cell range

See preview

4 Check the Series and Data range settings

5 Work through the options

5 Step 3: Add titles and make changes to the legend (key), axes or other aspects by clicking the relevant tabs.

6 Step 4: Place the chart on a separate sheet or accept the default to keep it with the original data.

Legend

6 Decide where the chart should go

Take note

The X-axis in a column chart is the *horizontal* axis, and the Y-axis is the *vertical* axis.

Tip

You can create a chart instantly by selecting the data and pressing [F11].

Amending and printing charts

1 Use the Chart toolbar options, e.g. to delete the legend, change chart type or angle selected text.

2 To open the Format dialog box and amend colours, fonts, number styles, alignment, etc. of an element, right-click on it and select Format from the short menu; or use the Chart toolbar to select the element then click the Format button.

3 Right-click the data or chart area to add trend lines or amend the source data.

4 Select the chart to print it alone.

5 De-select to print it together with the spreadsheet data.

The chart appears 'selected' i.e. showing black squares (sizing handles) on the borders, and in this state it can be re-sized, moved or deleted in the same way as drawings or pictures. You can also format a selected chart using menu options or the chart toolbar – if this does not appear automatically, open it from the **View** > **Toolbars** menu. Clicking outside the chart de-selects it, and clicking inside will select it again.

Show/hide legend

Change chart type

Add table of data

Open Format dialog box

Alter data series

Select element

Angle text

2 Right-click and select Format

Tip

You often need to increase the size of the chart to see all the axes labels clearly.

Summary

❏ Spreadsheets are made up of hundreds of cells arranged in columns and rows. Cell addresses combine column heading letters and row heading numbers.

❏ You can use Excel to perform calculations, and the resultant data can be displayed in grids or used to create charts.

❏ Formulae always start with the equals sign and must be entered using correct operators. If they include cell addresses, rather than raw data, amending the data in the cell will result in an automatic update of your results.

❏ Text or numbers can be formatted to improve the appearance of the spreadsheet, and columns and rows can be inserted or deleted if you need to change your display. You can also add borders or shading or apply one of the design templates available.

❏ To save time, formulae can be copied across columns or rows as they make use of relative cell referencing. However, you need to make cell addresses absolute where these must remain constant.

❏ Spreadsheets can be printed with or without gridlines, small enough to fit one page and alone or with an accompanying chart.

❏ Charts are easy to produce using a Wizard. You just follow the steps and then format them in your preferred style.

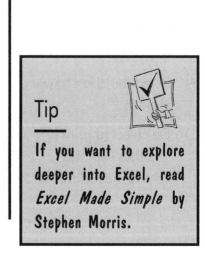

Tip

If you want to explore deeper into Excel, read *Excel Made Simple* by Stephen Morris.

6 Presentations

PowerPoint presentations

Everyone feels more comfortable giving talks when supported by good quality audiovisual aids. Using a presentation package such as Microsoft PowerPoint allows you to produce beautifully illustrated slides for printing on acetate sheets or running on the computer. They can include animation or sound effects and can be supported by various handouts and notes.

When you start PowerPoint, you will see a blank slide in the main pane of the Normal View, and will have two other areas available in which to work: the Outline tab where you can concentrate on typing your text, or the area below your slide where you can add some speaker's notes.

1 Click the PowerPoint icon 🖼 or select the application from the All Programs menu.

2 Click into a pane to start work on the blank slide.

Or

3 Start a new presentation from a template or a wizard.

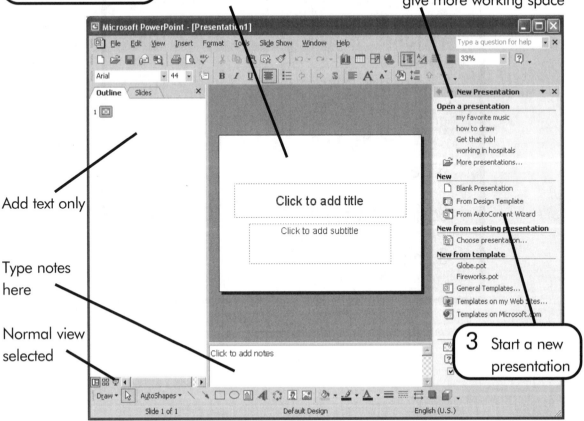

2 Click into a pane

Work on all aspects of a slide

Task Pane – close it to give more working space

Add text only

Type notes here

Normal view selected

3 Start a new presentation

Basic steps

Creating a presentation

1 To apply an alternative layout, go to Format > Slide Layout. Different examples of slide layouts will appear in the Task Pane.

2 Scroll down until you find a style you prefer.

3 Double-click or select the Apply option.

4 To add a new slide, select the Insert option.

Although you are offered a Title Slide when you open the program, there are a wide range of layouts available. Apart from the Blank layout, they offer different arrangements of 'placeholders' (specific areas already in place for adding charts, pictures or columns of text) to facilitate the design of your slide. Select an alternative or start with the slide that first appears.

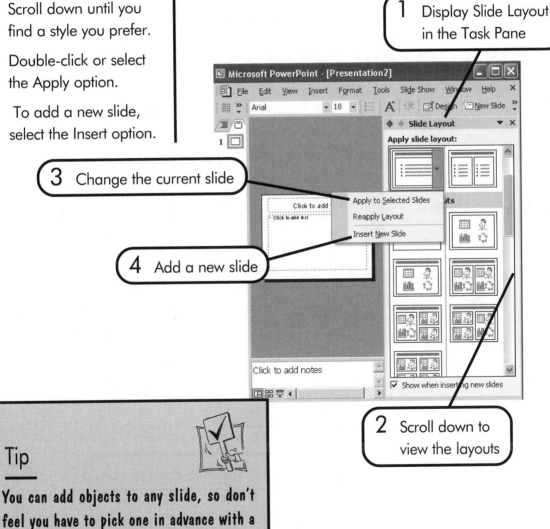

1 Display Slide Layout in the Task Pane

3 Change the current slide

4 Add a new slide

2 Scroll down to view the layouts

Tip

You can add objects to any slide, so don't feel you have to pick one in advance with a placeholder for charts or pictures.

Building up your slides

Once your first slide is in place, you can add others at any time. As you build up your slides, you will need to go between them and possibly change their order. You will also want to view them in different ways, to see how the whole presentation is looking.

□ To add a new slide

1 Click the New Slide toolbar button 🔲, or select this option from the Insert menu.

Or

2 On the Outline or Slides tab, click next to a slide and press [Enter].

3 Select a layout and apply it to your slide.

4 Continue adding slides until you have the correct number for your presentation.

5 To go between your slides, click the navigation arrows to the right of the slide.

1 Click New Slide

2 Click and press [Enter]

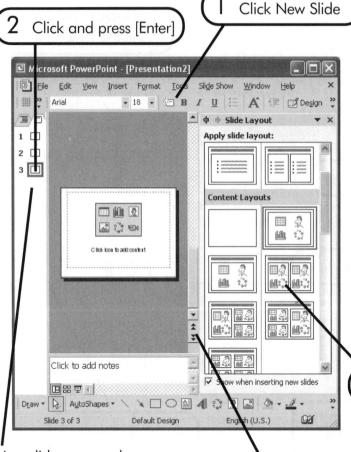

3 Click to apply a layout

New slide appears here

5 Click the arrows to change slides

Different views

❑ To change views

1 Click one of the toolbar View buttons or select from the View menu.

2 Select a slide.

3 In Normal view, drag the boundaries to change the size of the panes.

4 If you are watching a Slide Show, run through the presentation by pressing [Page Up] or [Page Down] or clicking the mouse. Exit by pressing [Esc].

There are three View toolbar buttons:

In **Normal** view, all three panes are visible on screen together. The Outline tab where you work on text alternates with the Slides tab showing thumbnails of your slides.

Use **Slide sorter** view to see the complete presentation on screen as thumbnails.

Use **Slide show** view to step through the presentation to see how it would look when run on a computer.

Select **View > Notes Page** to type in speaker's notes below a thumbnail of any slide, or **View > Master** to add text or objects that will appear on all your slides, notes or handouts.

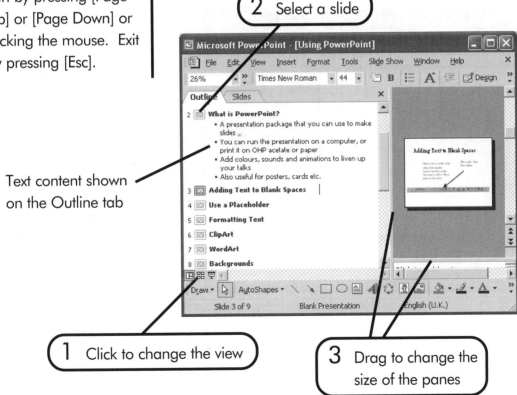

2 Select a slide

Text content shown on the Outline tab

1 Click to change the view

3 Drag to change the size of the panes

Tip

Moving or re-ordering slides is easy in Slide Sorter view. Just click the slide you wish to move and drag it to its new position, which will be marked by a dotted vertical line.

Slide Sorter view

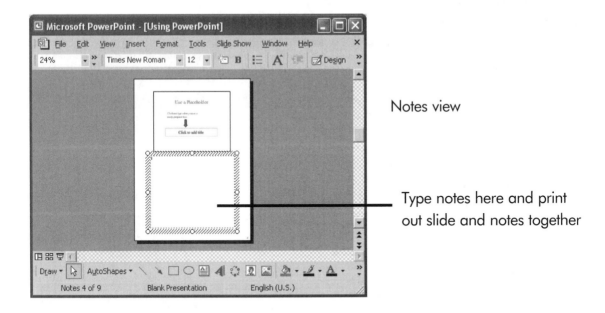

Notes view

Type notes here and print out slide and notes together

Basic steps

1 Click in the placeholder and enter text as usual. Press [Enter] to add a new line within the same box.

2 For blank slides or areas, click the Text Box button on the Drawing toolbar and then click in place on the slide.

3 Start typing in the box – it will expand to provide room for the text.

You have two options with text: using placeholders and clicking directly in the boxes provided, or adding a text box to any part of the slide.

To change the default formatting, select the text and then use the **Format** menu options or toolbar buttons just as you would in word processing.

There are some extra options that can be particularly useful:

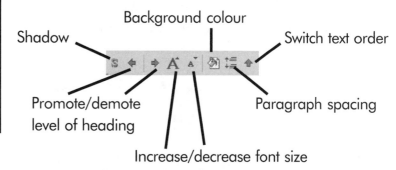

Shadow

Background colour

Switch text order

Promote/demote level of heading

Paragraph spacing

Increase/decrease font size

Title not yet entered

Text written on the slide is copied automatically into the Outline pane

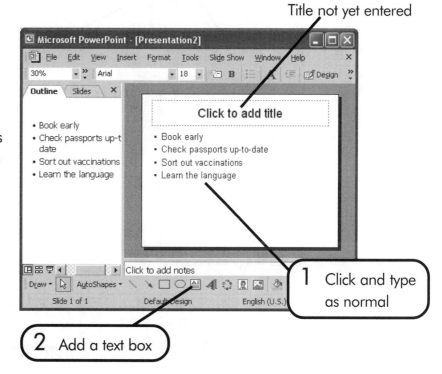

1 Click and type as normal

2 Add a text box

Altering text boxes

Text boxes used in PowerPoint do not usually have borders showing when you have completed text entry. If these appear and aren't wanted, remove them by selecting the box border, click the **Line Color** button and select **No Line**.

Otherwise, enhance the slide by choosing from a wide range of colours, widths and style of line to surround your text. You can also change the size of the text box and move it to different parts of the slide by clicking to show the sizing handles and dragging with a 2-way arrow (to re-size) or 4-way arrow (to move).

1 To select a text box, click on the text to pick up an invisible box, then click on one of the box edges.

2 A selected text box has a thick, textured edge with sizing handles around it.

3 Use the Drawing toolbar options to change its lines and backgrounds (fill).

Fill effects – colours, textures and patterns

Line Color – includes No Line   Line width   Line style

Before…

…and after

Sizing handle

Text can get lost on a fussy background!

Basic steps

1 Click the Word Art button on the Drawing toolbar.

2 Select a style from the WordArt Gallery.

3 Click OK.

4 In the editing box, type in your text.

5 Select the font and size, and set bold or italic if wanted.

6 Click OK.

cont...

Although you can change font types, styles, colours and sizes in normal text boxes, you can have more fun with words if you create them in Word Art.

These words can be shaped, stretched, shaded and blocked and given unusual colour effects. They are very useful for pasting across your slide at angles, or for special-effect titles.

2 Select a WordArt style

3 Click OK

5 Define the font, size and style

4 Enter your text

6 Click OK

Tip

Clip art images can be inserted, just as in Word (see page 44).

105

The WordArt appears on the slide

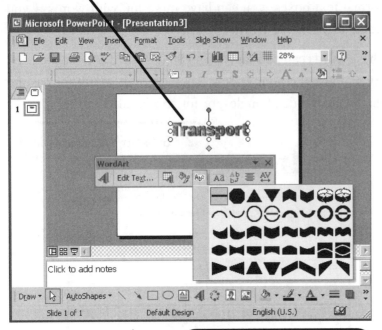

cont...

❑ The text will appear on your slide with the colour and shape you originally selected, together with the WordArt toolbar. Click and drag on the text to move it into position.

7 Make changes to orientation, spacing between letters, shading, colour or alignment, change the shape of the words or return to the gallery to find an alternative.

8 Click outside the text to accept it, or select the text to re-open the WordArt toolbar.

7 Adjust the appearance

Gallery   Shape   Align

Spacing between letters

Format   Letter height   Vertical text

8 Click outside to accept it

Tip

Use the yellow diamond shaped handle to adjust the curvature, depth or other key feature of the WordArt.

Basic steps

1 Double-click the Chart placeholder or click the toolbar button.

2 Select Organization Chart from the Diagram Gallery.

3 Click into a box to enter your own text. Use the normal formatting tools to change its appearance.

4 To remove an unwanted box, select it and press [Delete].

5 Return to your slide by clicking outside the chart area.

Charts and other objects

PowerPoint has access to a range of applications that can add visual effects to your slides. Some of these are available directly from placeholders or from the **Insert** menu, for others you need to **Insert > Object** and scroll through the applications listed.

Organization Charts

This application allows you to present hierarchical information such as family trees or company management structures. You design the chart using the Organization Chart toolbar.

1 Start from a placeholder or the toolbar button

2 Select Organization Chart

3 Type and format your text

Customising an Organization Chart

You can insert extra boxes to build up your hierarchy by adding new members e.g. assistants or subordinates. You will also find a gallery of styles to let you apply different colours and borders to your chart to enhance its appearance.

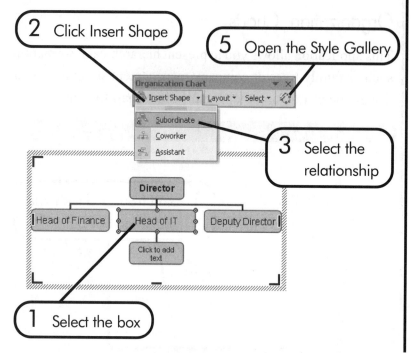

2 Click Insert Shape

5 Open the Style Gallery

3 Select the relationship

1 Select the box

- ❑ To add a new box

1 Click the box where you want to add a new member.

2 On the toolbar, click Insert Shape.

3 Find the appropriate relationship and select it. A new box will appear on your chart.

- ❑ Formatting

4 Right-click and select Format>Organisation Chart to add back-ground colours or borders.

5 Open the Style Gallery to apply a new style.

The Style Gallery offers a range of alternative designs

108

Basic steps

1 Double-click a place-holder showing a chart, click the toolbar button or select Insert > Chart to take you to the chart application.

2 Click on the datasheet to enter your own text and numbers, and delete unwanted cells.

3 To change the chart type, select from Chart – Chart Type and preview the effect of the change before clicking OK.

4 To insert or to format the fonts, alignment, legend (key), colours of lines etc., right-click on the relevant data, axis or title and select from the shortcut menu.

5 To return to your slide, click once *outside* the chart. To return for amendments, double-click the chart itself.

Numerical charts

To display numerical data visually, you can use one of the charting applications available from PowerPoint, e.g. Microsoft Graph. Replace the sample data and edit or format the chart to insert it into your presentation.

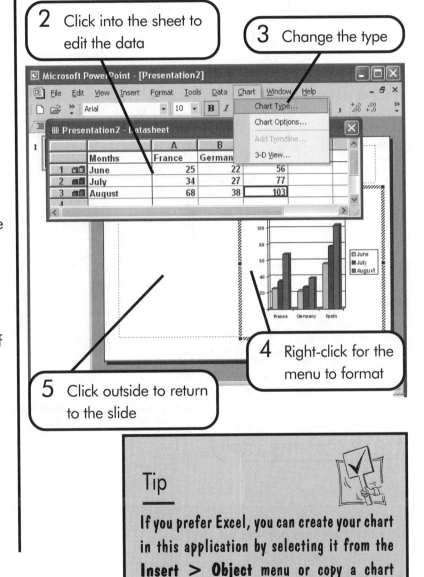

2 Click into the sheet to edit the data

3 Change the type

4 Right-click for the menu to format

5 Click outside to return to the slide

Tip

If you prefer Excel, you can create your chart in this application by selecting it from the Insert > Object menu or copy a chart across from Excel using Copy and Paste.

Slide design

Rather than have a white background for your slides, you can add colours, patterns and special features or use one of the design templates available. You can also decide whether to have a different design for each slide, or standardise your presentation and give every slide the same 'look'.

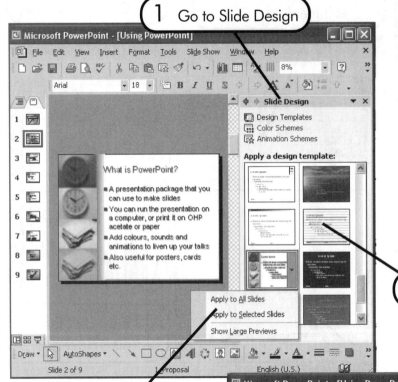

1 Go to Slide Design

2 Preview the designs

3 Select an Apply option

The title slide has one design; a second design has been applied to all the rest

Basic steps

Customising slide designs

You can add coloured or textured backgrounds or apply a complete colour scheme that combines text, background and fill colours as a united theme.

❑ Background

1 Open the Format menu and select Background.

2 Select a colour or click More Colors... for a wider choice.

Or

3 Click Fill Effects... to use textures, gradients, patterns or pictures.

❑ Colour Schemes

4 Select Color Schemes in the Slide Design Task Pane and apply one to all or selected slides.

5 To change elements, click Edit and clear the check boxes.

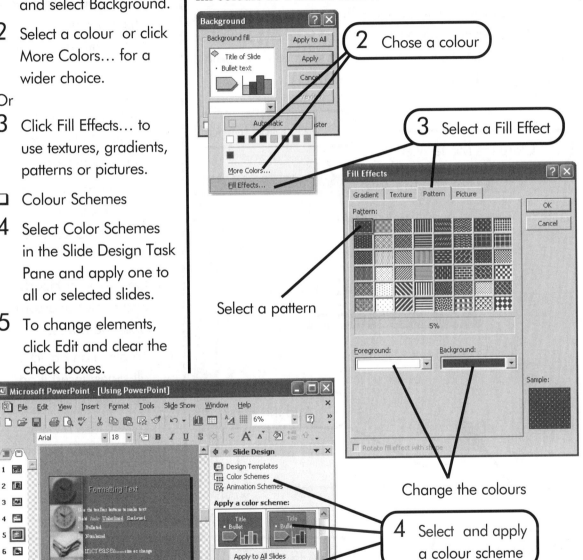

2 Chose a colour

3 Select a Fill Effect

Select a pattern

Change the colours

4 Select and apply a colour scheme

5 Edit the scheme

Slide Master

The *Slide Master* controls the basic features of your slides such as the text formatting or background. It also contains placeholders for titles and main text, dates, footers and slide numbers This means that, if you want to change bullet styles or include a logo or the date on every slide, you don't need to amend each slide in turn. Make the changes to the master slide and your whole presentation will be updated automatically.

1 Go to View > Master > Slide Master.

2 Select and format the title or lower levels of text in the normal way.

3 Click on the text and select Format > Bullets and Numbering to change bullet styles for the presentation.

4 To add dates or slide numbers to all slides, use the marked areas.

Or

5 Click View > Header and Footer and complete the boxes.

6 To place an object on all slides, insert it on the Slide Master.

7 Click Close Master View to return to the slide, or click the Normal view button.

7 Close the Master View

2 Select and format

4 Add the date?

6 Add an image to all slides?

5 Add a footer?

Saving and printing

1 Save presentations in the normal way by completing the Save As dialog box with the name of the file and location.

2 Go to File > Page Setup to select the orientation and size.

3 Select File > Print for any printing options other than one copy of all the slides.

4 Choose whether to print slides, handouts, notes or an outline.

5 Select the arrangement of images on your handouts.

Once you have done any work on a presentation, you need to save it. You should save regularly so that you maintain an updated version of the presentation.

A single presentation file contains all the slides, outlines, notes etc. that you have prepared, and you save it in exactly the same way as you save Word documents.

Printing is different as you can choose what you print, and you will need to set the appropriate orientation and size from the **Page Setup** dialog box.

2 Set the size and orientation

4 Choose what to print

5 Handout layout?

Tip

If printing for overhead projectors, make sure the acetate sheets are suitable for your printer.

Summary

❑ With PowerPoint you can produce slides and supporting material to enhance your presentations.

❑ You can run a slide show on the computer or print onto overhead projector transparencies or paper.

❑ New slides can be selected from a range of layouts, but you can change these as you work and start with a blank slide if you prefer.

❑ Change the view to see the outline text, notes pages, full slides or all the slides as thumbnails, or to view the slide show.

❑ Placeholders make it easy to add text, charts or pictures to your slides. Objects can be added to any slide and moved or re-sized if necessary.

❑ Organization charts and other diagrams can easily be created using the Diagram Gallery.

❑ As well as the usual text formatting tools, there are extra facilities to enable you to add special effects, and WordArt is a different type of text you can include.

❑ To give your presentation a uniform look, apply one design to all the slides and use the Master slide to include the same text or image on every slide.

❑ When printing, you can produce slides, notes, handouts or just the text outline of your presentation.

Tip

If you want to get more out of PowerPoint, read *PowerPoint Made Simple* by Moira Stephens, and for a fuller introduction to the Office suite, try *Office XP Made Simple* by P.K.McBride.

7 The Internet

Getting connected

If your computer has a modem – a piece of hardware that enables you to connect to the Internet via a normal telephone line – you will be able to find information and communicate via the international network of computers known as the Internet.

The World Wide Web

Often referred to as the Web, this is the name given to the linked multimedia documents that have been loaded onto the Internet and that offer anything from film clips, medical articles, stock market information and weather reports to goods and services you can buy without leaving your own home.

Connecting

To connect to the Internet and search the Web, you need an Internet Access or Service Provider (ISP) and the software to view Web pages, known as a *browser*. Today, some ISPs charge a monthly fee that includes a set number of free hours online, but the majority offer a free connection and you pay for all the phone calls. You should find ISP CD-ROMs in shops or magazines. Follow the instructions on the CD-ROM and you will install all the software you need, including one of the two well-known browsers – Netscape or Internet Explorer.

1 **Double-click the ISP or browser icon on your Desktop or click your connection icon and then click Dial.**

2 **You may see a Web page from your ISP.**

3 **A small computer icon will be seen flashing on the Taskbar to show you are connected to the Internet.**

Tip

Where access to the Internet is free, watch the clock when seeking technical support by telephone, as you can be charged over 50p per minute.

1 Double-click the browser icon to connect

Internet Explorer

Basic steps

1 To finish working on the Internet altogether, close the browser window to open the Disconnect dialog box and click Disconnect Now.

2 To keep the present page on screen but go 'offline', double-click the computer icon on the Taskbar and click the Disconnect button.

Saving money

As you are likely to pay for every minute you are linked to the Internet, you should work offline as much as possible to keep costs down. If you have accessed a long document you want to read at your leisure, or when you have finished working on the Internet, disconnect to close the telephone connection. You can always reconnect again if you want to access a new site or send or receive messages.

Message you may get when you close the Browser window

1 Click Disconnect Now

Message box when you double-click the computer icon or open Dial up

2 Click Disconnect

Web pages

Both browsers have similar menus and toolbar buttons, and these will be visible all the time. In the main window you will see the opening Web page known as the 'home page'. Each service provider has its own home page appearing by default, and you will return to this page whenever you click the Home toolbar button.

Basic steps

❑ To show button labels

1 Open the View menu, point to Toolbars and select Customize…

2 In the Text options box select Show text labels.

Stop downloading

Forward to page you came back from

Reload page

Go to your Home page

Shortcuts to favourite sites

Go to previous page

Sites you have visited

Web page address

Close browser

Print page

Take note

Web pages are written in **HTML** (HyperText Markup Language) and are known as html files.

Tip

If you find a page you want to start all your online sessions from, use **Tools > Internet Options** and on the **General** tab click *Use Current Page* in the **Home Page** area.

Using hyperlinks

Take note

The Home Page toolbar button takes you to the page you always open when you connect to the Internet. On a Web page, clicking a Home hyperlink will normally take you to the main index or opening page for that site.

As you move the mouse pointer over a Web page, it will keep changing from the normal arrow to a hand ☜. Whenever this happens, it means the text or image on which it is resting is a hyperlink. It can be 'clicked' and will then link to another page on the Web. Hyperlink text is often blue and underlined, and changes colour after clicking.

If a hyperlink takes you to a page of no interest, return to the original page by clicking the *Back* toolbar button. Change your mind and *want* to go to that page after all – click the Forward toolbar button to make the link again.

Click here...

...to open this page

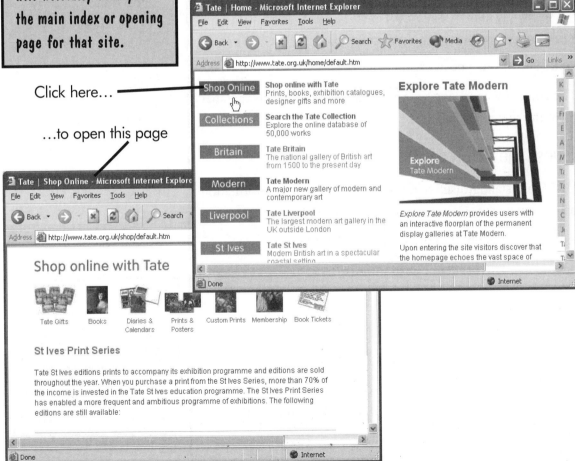

119

Addresses and URLs

The address of any Web page is known as its Uniform Resource Locator (URL). Each URL has several sections and the punctuation between these MUST be entered accurately, although text can be either upper or lower case. For example, the BBC Home Page can be reached by entering

> http://www.bbc.co.uk

http:// is short for hypertext transfer protocol, and means the file is a hypertext document (Web page). You may see other codes on the Web, e.g. **ftp://** for file transfer protocol, that indicates a site from which files can be downloaded.

www. denotes the World Wide Web

bbc is the company name

co.uk shows the type of organisation, i.e. a company in the UK.

The company name and type of organisation elements together form the *domain name*.

Guess the address

URLS are standardised and you are given certain information by the extension. Common extensions include:

.com   US and international companies

.ac.uk   UK academic institutions

.edu   American universities and colleges

.gov.uk   governmental sites in the UK

.org.uk   organizations such as charities, in the UK.

This system means that you can sometimes guess the address for an organization if you know its name, location and the type of business.

1 Type the URL into the Address box and press [Enter].

2 Check that the browser logo is revolving to show the connection is being made.

3 If it seems to be taking too long for the page to download, click the Stop button and try again later.

Tip

You don't usually need to type http:// — just start with www.

120

The best ways to search

1 Connect to the URL for
   the directory, e.g.
   www.excite.co.uk

2 Click first choice of
   category heading.

3 As lists appear, scroll
   down and click on the
   most appropriate
   heading.

A major role for the Web is to provide information. As you can't know the exact location of every Web page holding relevant information, you will need the help of a directory or search engine at some stage. Many organisations offer both types of search on the same site, and popular URLs include www.altavista.com, www.ukdirectory.co.uk, www.google.com, www.yahoo.co.uk, www.excite.co.uk and www.hotbot.com.

Directories

Directories work like a book contents page or library classification system. The companies examine and classify Web pages under various headings and subheadings. You just need to click on a category and work down through the lists that keep appearing until you reach actual Web sites to browse through. Often you have the chance to enter a specific word or phrase to carry out a search within a particular sub-category.

Take note

Although thousands of sites may be listed, they are often arranged alphabetically 10 - 15 per page, and so it is easy to reach the appropriate listings.

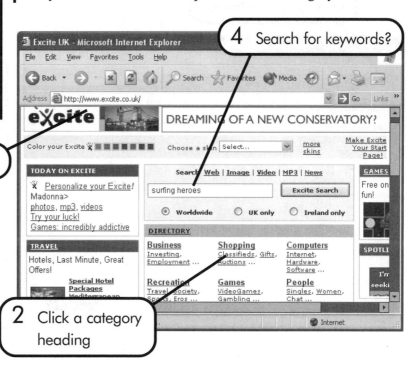

4 Search for keywords?

1 Enter the URL

2 Click a category heading

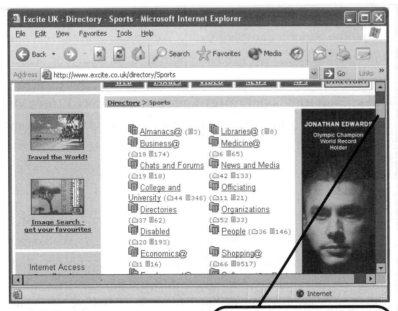

5 Scroll through the list

6 Go back to the list

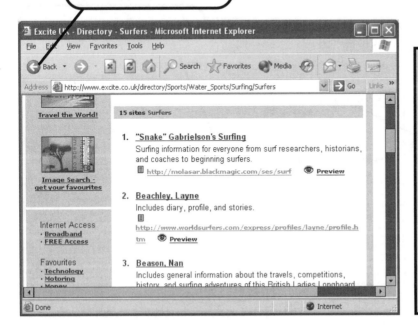

4 At any stage, enter *keywords* if a box is provided to make a search of this sub-category. A 'keyword' is any word or a phrase that describes what you are searching for.

5 When you reach the list of Web sites, page through.

6 Click any of interest, and use the Back button to return to the results list.

Take note

Related Web pages transferred together onto the Internet form a *Web site*. The main address followed by / and then more information shows the exact page you are visiting on site.

Search engines

1 Connect to the URL.

2 Click in the search box and enter your key-words and symbols carefully.

3 Click the Search button (this may be labelled Go, Seek or Search), or press [Enter].

4 Work down through the list of Web sites pro-vided and, after visiting any, return to the list using the Back button.

Search engines build up huge databases of Web pages and you instruct them to carry out searches by matching *keywords* you type into a special box – the query box.

The result is often vast lists of pages, but these start with the most relevant and each 'hit' will show the first line of contents and when the page was last updated, to help you decide whether to download and examine it in more detail.

1 Go to the site

2 Enter the keywords

3 Click Search

Number of pages found

4 Work through the results

Rules when searching:

- Type a phrase between quotation marks so that words are not searched independently, e.g. "Christmas Island" to avoid Christmas-based sites.

- Use logical operators or + or - signs so that a search will find sites that:

  Must contain all words joined by AND e.g. gardens AND Hampshire

  Can contain either word linked by OR

  Will be excluded if any words follow AND NOT

  Must contain words prefixed by +

  Must not contain words prefixed by -

Tip

Avoid capital letters unless looking for proper names. You can use either case, but text in capitals may only be matched exactly. Spelling is also important as the search is for matching words.

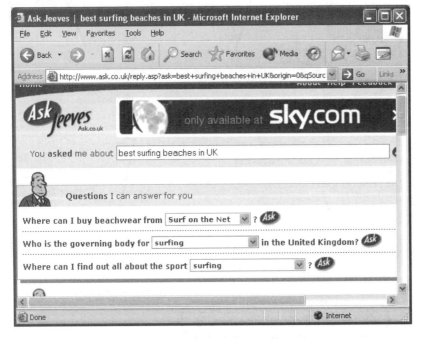

At some sites you can type in naturally worded questions – these are not generally the best way to get an exact match!

Favourite pages

❑ Adding Favorites

1 When you want to store the address of a Web page, click Favorites.

2 Click Add... to open the Add Favorite dialog box.

3 Accept or amend the name so that you will recognise it when searching for it in future. (Automatic entries are often much too long or meaning-less).

4 Click on a folder for your page in the Create In area, or create and name a new folder to hold it.

5 Click OK.

❑ To go to a favourite page, open the Favorites menu, open the folder and click on the page name.

After some time online, you may come across a Web page that you know you will want to revisit. Rather than write down the exact URL on a piece of paper, you can save it into the browser's special filing system. This is known as *Favorites* in Internet Explorer and *Bookmarks* in Netscape.

Next time you want to access the page, open the Favorites menu, click the name and you will be taken directly to the page you 'bookmarked'.

1 Click Favorites

2 Click Add...

3 Edit the name

5 Click OK

4 Select or create the folder

Organizing Favorites

To organize favourites, if they have been stored haphazardly, you can either use the folders provided (which may already contain links included by your ISP), or create your own.

3 Click Organize...

2 Drag or use the menu options

6 Click Move to Folder

4 Open the folder

5 Select a link

7 Delete or rename?

8 Click Close

1 Click the Favorites toolbar button.

2 Drag the favorite to another folder or right-click and select an option from the menu.

Or

3 Click Organize...

4 Scroll down to find the folder in which one was stored.

5 Select a favorite link.

6 To move it to a different folder, click Move to Folder and select the new destination folder in the window.

7 Choose other options if you want to delete or rename the page or create a new folder.

8 Click Close.

Tip

To add the current page to your Favorites hold [Control] and press [D].

126

Going shopping

What do you want to buy today? A book, theatre tickets, holidays or a house? You can buy almost anything on the Internet nowadays, and it can be safe and much less tiring than walking round a real shopping centre.

As with any purchase, you must take certain precautions:

- Check the company exists – is there an address and phone number to contact them if you have a problem?

- Find out what they charge for delivery.

- Phone up the company when paying, if you don't trust the security system for taking credit card details on-line.

- Make sure goods bought from overseas will work in the UK, e.g. are the videos the right type for your machine?

Research shows that people are often happiest dealing with companies with a high street presence or experience in the distribution of goods, but if you want to take the risk you could get a real bargain with a small, unknown organisation.

Sainsburys – having heavy shopping delivered can be a luxury worth far more than the £5 delivery charge. Go to www.sainsburys.co.uk and register your details, then browse the aisles, adding items to your trolley. When ready, place your order, select the delivery slot and wait for the doorbell.

Printing Web pages

If you find a Web page you want to print, you can treat it in a similar fashion to a Word document. However, the length of a Web 'page' does not correspond to that of a word processed document, and may extend over several printed pages.

Many Web pages are divided into sections – *frames* – that comprise separate pages displayed in a special way. You need to take care when printing these to make sure you end up with the information you want.

5 Set the print range

4 Only print the frame?

Basic steps

1 To print one copy of the complete Web page, click the Print toolbar button.

2 To print a frame, click it first.

3 To change settings, go to File > Print.

4 For one frame, click Options and choose to print *Only the selected frame*.

5 To print only the first section of a long Web page, set the print range to Pages from 1–1.

☐ Saving images

1 Right-click the image and select the Save Picture As… option.

2 Leave the default file type, *jpg or gif*, or save it as a bitmap *(bmp)*.

3 Give it a name you will remember and click Save.

☐ Desktop

4 Select Set As Background to use the picture as your Desktop background – it will be centred, tiled or stretched depending on your display settings.

5 Return to normal via the Start > Control Panel > Display > Desktop menu.

You save a Web page just like other documents. It will be saved as an html file and will open in the browser window. Images on Web pages may need to be saved separately as they are files in their own right.

1 Right-click and select Save Picture As…

4 Select Set as Background

3 Name it and click Save

2 Change the type?

Any picture can be used as background

Downloading files

New versions of software, games or special Internet tools found on the Web can all be transferred and saved onto your computer by a process known as *downloading*. It can take a long time to complete the transfer, so you are best downloading at cheap rate times. Programs are often free, or trial versions which you pay for if you keep them permanently.

Follow downloading guidelines and stay connected to the Internet during transfer. At the end, you may need to restart your computer before you can use the new programs. You can usually choose a particular folder into which the files will be downloaded, and whether to place an icon on your Desktop offering a shortcut to the program.

1 Go to the site where the file is located, e.g. www.canon-europa.com

2 Click the hyperlink to start the download – it may just say <u>Click here</u>.

3 Accept the suggested location, or choose a folder in which to store your program.

4 A dialog box may be displayed showing the status of the transfer.

1 Go to the site

Canon Europa - Software Downloads - Microsoft Internet Explorer
File   Edit   View   Favorites   Tools   Help

Back

Address http://www

Canon

Imaging across networks

About Canon
Support
Products
Canon News
Sponsorship
Contact Canon
Canon Sites

I agree to the

2 Follow the download instructions

25% of b1a51ukx.e

Saving:
b1a51ukx.exe from www.canon-europa.com

Estimated time left 14 min 50 sec (580 KB of 2.31 MB copied)
Download to: C:\Program Files\Canon\b1a51ukx.exe
Transfer rate: 2.42 KB/Sec

☐ Close this dialog box when download completes

Open   Open Folder   Cancel

4 Watch and wait

Take note

Commonly downloaded files include updated drives for printers and scanners, image editors e.g. *Paintshop Pro,* **Web page authoring programs e.g.** *FrontPage Express* **and software that allows you to transfer your own pages onto the Web e.g.** *CuteFTP.*

What is e-mail?

E-mail is short for electronic mail and is a cheap and quick method for sending messages to other computer users via the Internet. Large documents or pictures can be sent in the form of attachments to your messages, and all you pay is a local phone charge.

Advantages over the post ('snail mail') or telephone:

- Messages sent to other countries arrive within minutes.

- No need to be at home – messages wait in a distant mailbox until you download them onto your computer.

- You'll never need to buy stamps or go to the postbox.

E-mail addresses

You will need an e-mail address of your own, assigned when you register with an e-mail service, and the address of the person receiving your message. An e-mail address is made up of the following parts:

User name – this is chosen by you and is usually a nickname or combination of initials and surname, e.g. *z.nobody*

Mail server – the computer where your messages are held, *e.g. virgin.net*

These two parts are separated by @ so that the full address looks like this: *z.nobody@virgin.net*

Tip
There are no full, reliable e-mail directories, but you can use Internet 'people' searches or online directories to try to find an individual or business address.

Take note
You have to be 100% accurate when typing an e-mail address or your messages will be returned unsent.

Outlook Express

The examples in this book relate to Microsoft Outlook Express version 6, but most e-mail systems work in a similar way. When you open the software the main choices are:

- Opening an **Inbox** and viewing new messages;

- . **Replying** to someone, or **forwarding** incoming messages to someone else;

- **Composing** new messages to send;

- Maintaining lists of addresses in your **Address Book**;

- Creating **folders** in which to store messages;

- **Attaching** a file to a message;

- **Deleting** unwanted messages.

1 Double-click the icon for your e-mail application to open the main window. This has toolbar options, tips and short cuts.

2 Click the Inbox folder to view your messages. (New users normally find a welcome message from their access provider.)

3 Select a message to see its contents in the lower preview pane.

4 To alter the size of a pane, drag its border when the pointer is a two-way arrow.

5 To alter the layout, use View > Layout... and select the elements to include.

1 Open the e-mail application

2 Go to the Inbox

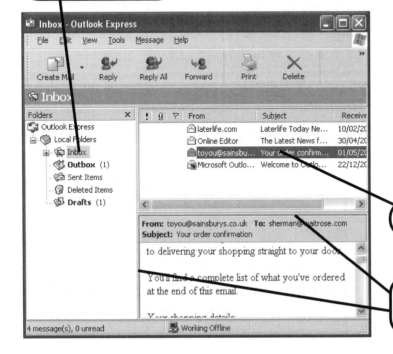

3 Select a message

4 Drag the borders to adjust the sizes

Basic steps

1 Click the Create Mail button or use Message > New Message.

2 Insert the recipient(s) addresses and the Subject.

3 Write your message.

4 Apply formatting and spell check it by clicking the Spelling button.

5 For an urgent message, select Priority > High. This will attach an exclamation mark to it.

6 Click Send to send it straight away, or select File > Send Later to retain it in the Outbox.

Tip

Take care when entering the Subject. Well-worded, it can ensure that your message stands out from many others that may be received and will be read rather than ignored.

Sending messages

To send a message, open a composing window and enter:

● The e-mail address of the recipient in the *To* box;

● The addresses of anyone receiving a copy in the *Cc.* box;

● The address of anyone who will receive a copy of the message unknown to other recipients – a blind copy – in the *Bcc.* box. (To use this box in Outlook Express you need to open it by selecting **View** > **All Headers**.)

● The subject of the message in the *Subject* box;

● The message itself, in the lower message box.

Either send your message straight away or keep it to send later when you go online.

In Outlook Express, messages are stored in the Outbox and, after sending, are listed in the Sent box.

2 Insert the relevant information

6 Click Send

5 Assign priority?

4 Format and spell check

3 Write the message

Receiving messages

When you open Outlook Express, download new messages into your Inbox by clicking the Send/Receive and then the Connect buttons. Once messages appear, go offline to read and reply to them at your leisure.

For each message, you see exactly who sent it and when, and can print a hard copy if you want one. Each selected message opens in the preview pane, but double-click to open it fully.

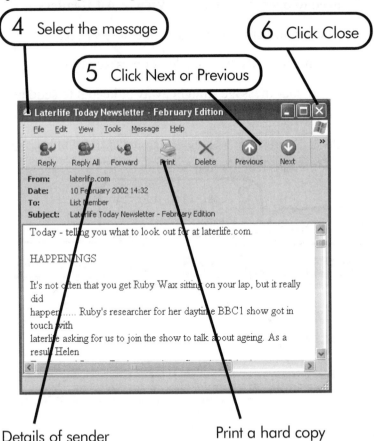

Details of sender

Print a hard copy

1 Click the Send/Receive button to connect to your mail server and download any new messages waiting for you.

2 The number of messages will be displayed in brackets next to the Inbox.

3 If the Inbox is not your default opening screen, click this choice in the Folders pane to open it and view the messages.

4 Select a message to read in preview or open fully.

5 After reading the message, use Next or Previous buttons to read other messages.

6 Close its window with the Close button.

1 Select the incoming message and click the Reply button ⚑. A composing window will open showing the To: box completed and the Subject: box starting *Re:* followed by the original subject.

2 Partially or fully delete the original message, or leave as a reminder.

3 Click in the space at the top of the message box and type in your reply.

4 Complete and send exactly as you would any original message.

To reply to the author of a message, using the **Reply** function will automatically enter their address and give you the chance to retain some or all the original message in your own reply.

Forward a message to a third person by clicking the **Forward** button ⚑ and complete the message box as normal. The Subject box will include the original subject prefixed by *Fw:* but you will need to enter the new e-mail address yourself.

To: and Subject completed for you

4 Complete and send

Re: Laterlife Today Newsletter - February E...

File   Edit   View   Insert   Format   Tools   Message   Help

Send   Cut   Copy   Paste   Undo   Check

To: laterlife-feedback-14@lb.bcentral.com

Cc:

Subject: Re: Laterlife Today Newsletter - February Edition

I noticed in this month's newsletter that you didn't mention Gladys King's new book on retirement.

Can you add the details next time?

Many thanks.

----- Original Message -----
From: "laterlife.com"

3 Type your reply

2 Edit the original message

Tip

If you are one of a number of people sent a message and want everyone on the mailing list to receive a copy of your reply, click the *Reply All* button rather than the *Reply* button. The e-mail addresses of the whole group will be included in the *To:* box.

Attaching files

Although you can use basic formatting tools, you can't send beautifully word-processed e-mail messages, or insert pictures. Instead, you should attach these as files created and saved elsewhere. They will remain in their original state and will be opened by your message recipient into an application.

☐ Attaching a file

1 Click the Attach button or select Insert > File Attachment.

2 In the Insert Attachment dialog box, browse through your folders and select the file you want to send.

3 Click the Attach button. The filename will be shown in a new Attach box.

4 Repeat the process to attach several files to a single message.

5 To delete an attach-ment, select it and press [Delete].

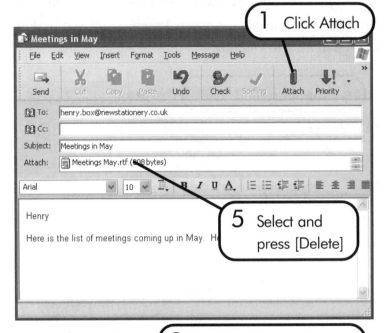

1 Click Attach

5 Select and press [Delete]

2 Browse and select the file

3 Click Attach

Tip

You can attach files from within a program or on the Desktop. Right-click or go to File > Send To > Mail Recipient. Select the Compress option first to zip large files.

136

Basic steps

Opening attachments

1 Look for the paperclip icon next to a message that shows there is an attachment.

2 Select the message.

Either

3 Click the paperclip in the top right-hand corner of the preview pane, then click on the filename.

Or

4 Double-click the filename showing in the Attach box after opening the message fully.

5 Click Save Attachments to save it elsewhere.

Messages with attachments display a paperclip icon. Open the attached file to view it, or save it if you want to transfer it to a different machine or keep it with related files.

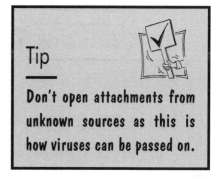

Take note

To insert text or images into the body of a message, use the options on the Insert menu.

Tip

Don't open attachments from unknown sources as this is how viruses can be passed on.

The Address Book

It would be quite annoying if you had to enter the same details every time you sent a message, and so you are saved the trouble by being able to build up an Address Book of e-mail addresses. You can also organise group mailing lists so that entering the group name inserts all the separate addresses at once.

1 Open the Address Book

2 Select New > New Contact

5 Store other details?

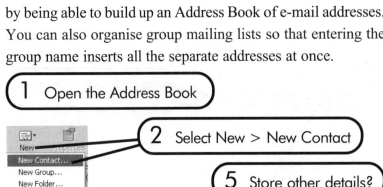

3 Give the name and e-mail address

4 Edit the display name

6 Click OK

1 In the Outlook Express window, click the Addresses button or select Tools > Address Book.

2 Click New and select New Contact.

3 Complete the name and e-mail details and click Add. The address will appear in the main window.

4 Accept or amend the name to be displayed.

5 Click other tabs to store more information.

6 Click OK.

❑ To group several addresses under a single heading, select New > New Group.

Tip

You can add the address of anyone who sends you a message, by right-clicking their name and selecting Add To Address Book from the menu.

1 Click 🖭To: or 🖭Cc: to open the Address Book.

2 Select a person or group name in the left pane.

3 Click the To:, Cc: or Bcc: buttons to enter the address into the appropriate message box.

4 Click OK and you will return to your message.

5 To delete an address, open the Address Book, select the name and click Delete.

6 To edit an address, select it and click the Properties button.

Once you have built up a list of e-mail addresses in your Address Book, you can enter these automatically into your new messages.

2 Select the name

3 Click To:, Cc: or Bcc:

4 Click OK

5 Select and click Delete

6 Select and click Properties

Organising messages

All new messages appear in your Inbox, but you should use existing folders or create new ones to store your messages systematically. Just as with file management, referring to a particular message is then much easier as you only need to look in a suitably named folder.

1 Right-click on the folder in which you want your new one to be created.

2 Select New Folder...

3 Enter the name for your new folder in the box.

4 Select the parent folder in the list and click OK.

5 Click the + next to a folder name to see its new subfolder.

1 Right-click on a folder

2 Select New Folder...

3 Enter a name

4 Click OK

5 Open the folder to see the new one

Basic steps

Moving messages

Either

1 Select the message.

2 Open the Edit menu or right-click and select Move to or Copy to Folder.

3 Select the destination folder, or create a new one first, and click OK.

Or

4 Display both the message and destination folder on the screen.

5 Drag the message across to the destination folder. (Hold down [Control] to copy but not move the original.)

6 When the folder becomes highlighted, let go of the mouse.

Tip

If you delete a message by mistake, open the *Deleted items* folder and drag the message out into another folder.

Once you have created folders in which to store your messages, you can file the messages you want to keep. You can also delete any you know you won't need by selecting them and clicking the Delete button.

141

Summary

- [ ] The Internet links computers around the world. Register with an ISP to access it via a modem and the telephone system, and view it through a browser.

- [ ] Web pages are written in a special code that allows you to click on text or images – a hyperlink – and link up with other pages. The address of any page is known as its URL.

- [ ] Searching the Web is aided by using directories or search engines. These allow you to search for keywords or to work through sites that have been grouped together under common headings.

- [ ] Whenever you find a page you will want to revisit, you can bookmark it by adding its URL to a list of links to favourite Web addresses.

- [ ] Shopping on the Internet is becoming as normal as mail order, and as long as you take sensible precautions, should be simple, safe and may save money.

- [ ] You can print and save pages and images from the Web, and you can download programs onto your PC.

- [ ] Once you have registered with an ISP, you can send e-mails around the world for the cost of a local phone call.

- [ ] Documents and images can be sent by e-mail as attached files.

- [ ] People's e-mail addresses can be saved into an Address Book and added to your messages automatically, and you can organise messages in folders just as you organise your own files.

Tip

If you want to know more about the Internet, read *The Internet Made Simple* by P.K. McBride.

Index